NOTES AND RECIPES FROM AN ISLAND KITCHEN

Rosalind Burgess

NOTES AND RECIPES FROM AN ISLAND KITCHEN

by

ROSALIND BURGESS

illustrated by

JUDITH MACLACHLAN

THOMAS & LOCHAR • NAIRN • SCOTLAND

British Library Cataloguing in Publication Data

Burgess, Rosalind
Notes and Recipes from an Island Kitchen
I. Title II. MacLachlan, J.
641.5

ISBN 0 946537 93 3

Typeset in Palatino, 11pt on 13pt by XL Publishing Services, Nairn, Scotland, and printed in Great Britain by J.W. Arrowsmith Ltd, Bristol

CONTENTS

FOREWORD

Rosalind Burgess is not only a very resourceful person but she has a frugal approach to the gifts of the natural world. Whether it is the *crotal* on the rocks which she uses to dye her wool or the seafood rich in nutrients for which she forages on the beach, everything is brought home to be put to good use.

Several summers ago friends of ours, a wine merchant and his French wife, came to stay in Skye. When we went to have lunch with them in the cottage they had rented on a sea loch almost everything we ate they had collected themselves. They had found chanterelles, ceps and boletus, wild berries, razorfish, mussels, cockles and small oysters and were revelling in all this food for free. It quite put us to shame.

This book is not a survival manual for those hoping to live entirely off the land nor does it suggest that we should all turn ourselves into full-time hunter-gatherers but many of its recipes remind us that there is still a rich harvest of wild things there for the taking from sea vegetables to salad leaves.

Cultivating a kitchen garden in the Hebrides has its downside: the rain and wind all too often destroy both crops and hopes, but as Skye's annual horticultural show triumphantly demonstrates the quality of the local soft fruit and the vegetables can be superb.

It is a quirky book this but practical; full of the kind of food that the author likes to cook for herself and her friends in her island kitchen; simple, fresh wholesome dishes and not a packet or a tin in sight.

You do not have to live on an island to enjoy fine food but for cooking to be pleasurable you must put a lot of love into it. Ask any great chefs what is the secret of their success and they will all tell you the same thing – a burning desire to cook but above all a respect for the taste and flavour of your raw materials. At a pinch dried herbs will do and so no doubt will canned carrots but, as Rosalind Burgess reaffirms in her approach to food, substituting the second best for the best is a recipe for disappointment. Anyone can turn out indifferent meals; really good food demands just a little bit more.

DEREK COOPER

FROM THE GARDEN

Living on an exposed peninsula overlooking the Outer Hebrides has made cultivating the garden an interesting and challenging endeavour, if not always one that is easy to achieve.

Fifteen years ago, filled with youthful optimism, a desire for self-sufficiency and a dream of, one day, looking through my kitchen window at rows of flourishing vegetables, I set to work with pick and spade, and, starting from a tiny patch just big enough to sow a crop of potatoes, extended the area not only to reach the length of the house but also to include a small enclosure for fruit bushes. Repeated fertilising using a large percentage of seaweed has greatly improved the soil, so that I can now successfully grow most root crops, a variety of brassicas, peas and beans, several different types of fruits and a good selection of herbs for both culinary and decorative purposes.

As most people who have gardens of their own will agree, there is little to match the joy of seeing the first green shoots poking through the ground, and, later savouring young vegetables pulled from the soil, then put straight into the pot or else scrubbed clean and eaten raw. In fact, being able to enjoy the benefits of my own produce most of the year round has given a great deal of pleasure, especially during the spring and summer months when the long daylight hours offer lots of good reasons for being outside, and when too much digging, weeding and grass cutting can seldom be considered a hardship.

Of course there are the less idyllic times, when a cold May wind blows all the blossom off the fruit bushes, or a midsummer gale flattens the tall-stemmed flowers and leaves the broad beans permanently leaning at a forty-five degree angle. These are indeed harrowing moments, which make me ask 'Is it all worthwhile?' but somehow, when spring returns, so does all the old optimism and enthusiasm, and I'm out there with my spade ready to repeat the cycle all over again!

So here are some ideas for soups, simple main courses, puddings, jams and chutneys which have been selected to use only the vegetables and fruits that I am able to grow, with the exception of the odd peppers, cucumbers and tomatoes which have been given to me by some kind friends who have a greenhouse.

CARROT AND PARSNIP SOUP *(Serves 4)*

225 g (½ lb) carrots
225 g (½ lb) parsnips
1 small onion
25 g (1 oz) butter
1.1 L (2 pints) chicken stock
1 bay leaf
3 strips finely pared orange peel
Salt and freshly ground pepper

Peel and slice the carrots, parsnips and onion. Melt the butter in a saucepan and add the vegetables. Cover and cook gently for 5 minutes. Pour on the stock and add the strips of orange peel, bay leaf and seasoning. Bring to the boil, and simmer for about 15 minutes or until vegetables are tender. Remove the bay leaf, and liquidise the soup. Check the seasoning and serve with a swirl of cream and a little chopped parsley.

CARROT AND TOMATO SOUP *(Serves 4)*

450 g (1 lb) carrots
225 g (½ lb) tomatoes
1 small onion
25 g (I oz) butter
1 bay leaf
1.1 L (2 pints) chicken stock
1 tbsp. fresh or 1 tsp. dried basil
Salt and freshly ground pepper

Melt the butter in a large saucepan and sauté the tomatoes, which have been roughly chopped. Add the peeled and sliced onion and carrots and continue cooking for 5 minutes; then, add the stock, bay leaf and the basil. Season with salt and pepper and simmer for 20 minutes. Liquidise, and serve with a spoonful of yoghurt and some chopped fresh basil.

ARTICHOKE SOUP *(Serves 4)*

450 g (1 lb) Jerusalem artichokes
1 onion
25 g (1 oz) butter
450 ml (¾ pint) milk
450 ml (¾ pint) chicken stock
Juice of ½ a lemon
¼ tsp. freshly ground nutmeg
Salt and freshly ground pepper

Scrub the artichokes, chop roughly and leave in a bowl of water to which a little vinegar has been added (this prevents the artichokes from discolouring).

Slice the onion and sauté it in the butter for about 5 minutes. Then, add the milk and the chicken stock. Bring to the boil, and simmer gently until the artichokes are soft. Liquidise the soup, and add the lemon juice, nutmeg and salt and pepper to taste.

Serve with croûtons or a sprinkling of crispy fried bacon.

BEETROOT SOUP *(Serves 4)*

This soup has a beautiful colour, and is made unusual by the spicy addition of cumin.

450 g (1 lb) raw beetroot
600 ml (1 pint) water
25 g (1 oz) butter
1 onion
175 g (6 oz) raw potato
300 ml (½ pint) milk
600 ml (1 pint) chicken stock
1 tsp. cumin seed
Juice of ½ a lemon
Salt and freshly ground black pepper

Wash the beetroot well and boil it in the water with ½ tsp. salt until tender. Remove the beetroot and peel off the skin; reserve the liquid.

Melt the butter in a pan, and gently sauté the chopped onion until transparent. Add the sliced potato and cook for a further 5 minutes. Then add the milk, stock and cumin and simmer slowly until the potato is cooked. Remove from the heat, add the chopped beetroot, together with the liquid they were cooked in, and then liquidise in a blender. Add lemon juice and seasoning to taste. Serve with a good spoonful of natural yoghurt and a sprinkling of chopped chives.

Herb and garlic rolls go well with this soup (see page 115).

SPINACH SOUP *(Serves 4)*

450 g (1 lb) fresh spinach
1 onion
1 potato
600 ml (1 pint) chicken stock
25 g (1 oz) butter
Salt and freshly ground pepper
A good pinch freshly ground nutmeg
Lemon juice to taste

Peel and chop the onion and potato and sauté with the butter in a large pan, without browning them, for about 5 minutes. Then, add roughly chopped spinach, the stock and salt and pepper, and simmer gently until the potatoes are tender. Liquidise in a blender and add the nutmeg and lemon juice. Serve with a good spoonful of yoghurt and some grated cheese.

This soup is best accompanied by crusty garlic bread (see page 114).

TURNIP AND RED PEPPER SOUP *(Serves 4)*

Turnip is a native to the islands, and grows in almost all types of soil. The addition of red pepper in this soup gives a fuller flavour.

1 medium-size turnip (swede)
1 onion
1 red pepper
25 g (1 oz) butter
1.1 L (2 pints) chicken stock
1 dsp. fresh or 1 tsp. dried sage
Salt and freshly ground pepper

Peel and dice the turnip, onion and red pepper. Melt the butter in a large pan and add the vegetables. Sauté gently for 5 minutes; then add the stock, sage and salt and pepper. Simmer for about 15 minutes or until the vegetables are tender. Liquidise in a blender, and serve with freshly chopped parsley and some thick slices of wholemeal bread (see page 109).

BRUSSELS SPROUT AND LEEK SOUP *(Serves 4)*

225 g (½ lb) Brussels sprouts
1 leek
25 g (1 oz) butter
300 ml (½ pint) milk
600 ml (1 pint) chicken stock
¼ tsp. nutmeg
Salt and freshly ground pepper

Wash and roughly chop the Brussels sprouts and the leek. Melt the butter in a saucepan, add the vegetables and sauté gently for 5 minutes. Then, add the milk and stock and bring to the boil, simmering gently for 15 minutes or until the vegetables are tender. Liquidise in a blender, add the nutmeg, and season to taste with salt and pepper.

Serve with croûtons.

LETTUCE, LOVAGE AND POTATO SOUP *(Serves 4)*

225 g (½ lb) lettuce thinnings or
1 cabbage lettuce
1 small onion
25 g (1 oz) butter
1 medium potato
600 ml (1 pint) chicken stock
300 ml (½ pint) milk
2-3 blades mace
1 dsp. fresh lovage
Salt and freshly ground pepper

Chop the onion and sauté in the butter, in a large saucepan, until transparent. Add the peeled and diced potato and cook gently for 5 minutes. Then, add the stock, milk, mace and chopped lovage. Simmer until the potato is almost cooked and then add the shredded lettuce. Continue cooking for a further 5 minutes, then remove from the heat, cool a little and liquidise.

Season with salt and pepper to taste and serve with croûtons.

FRESH PEA AND MINT SOUP *(Serves 4)*

450 g (1 lb) fresh peas
50 g (2 oz) butter
1 onion
1.1 L (2 pints) chicken stock
Several sprigs fresh mint
1 tsp. sugar
150 ml (¼ pint) single cream
Salt and freshly ground pepper

Melt the butter in a saucepan, add the chopped onion and cook gently for 5 minutes. Add the shelled peas, the stock and fresh mint, bring to the boil and simmer until the peas are tender. Add the sugar then remove the mint leaves and liquidise the soup, seasoning with salt and pepper to taste. Return to the saucepan, add the cream and heat gently, making sure not to boil.

Serve with a small sprig of mint in the centre of each bowl.

SCOTCH BROTH *(Serves 4)*

A nourishing Scotch broth may be served as the main part of a meal, and is a good way of using up the cheaper cuts of meat as well as any surplus vegetables in the garden.

675 g (1 ½ lb) neck of mutton
450 ml (¾ pint) water
1 medium onion
1 carrot (peeled)
1 small turnip (peeled)
1 leek
50 g (2 oz) pearl barley
1 bay leaf
Salt and freshly ground pepper
Freshly chopped parsley

Cut away any excess fat from the meat and then put it in a large saucepan together with the water and salt. Bring to the boil, then skim the surface and simmer gently for 1-2 hours. Leave to get cold and remove the fat with a slotted spoon.

Peel and finely slice the onion and dice the vegetables, adding to the stock together with the barley, bay leaf and a good grinding of pepper. Continue simmering for 20 minutes add the chopped parsley just before serving.

The meat can either be left on the bone and served as a cutlet or loosened into the broth with the bones discarded.

Celery, peas and shredded cabbage can all be used as a substitute or additional vegetable.

HEBRIDEAN SOLE FLORENTINE WITH MUSHROOM *(Serves 4–6)*

6 fillets Hebridean sole
600 ml (1 pint) milk and 150 ml (¼ pint) water
1 onion
1 bay leaf
Pinch of nutmeg
Salt and freshly ground pepper
675 g (1½ lbs) fresh spinach
50 g (2 oz) butter
225 g (½ lb) mushrooms
1 clove garlic

For the sauce:
50 g (2 oz) butter
50 g (2 oz) wholemeal flour
Stock in which the fish was cooked
½ tsp. mustard
Salt and freshly ground pepper
100 g (4 oz) mature cheddar cheese
Flaked almonds for garnish

Put the sole in a saucepan together with the water, milk, peeled and sliced onion, bay leaf, nutmeg and salt and pepper, and bring to the boil. Simmer gently until the fish is cooked, then strain and reserve the liquid. Put the spinach into a little boiling, salted water, cook until tender, and then strain well, roughly chop and place at the bottom of a buttered pie dish. Flake the fish, arrange over the top and keep warm.

Slice the mushroom, sauté in the butter, together with the crushed garlic, for 5 minutes and then remove them with a slotted spoon and sprinkle over the fish and spinach.

For the sauce: melt the butter in a saucepan, add the flour and cook for 1 minute. Slowly add the stock from the fish and, when thickened, add the mustard, salt and pepper and the grated cheese. Bring to the boil and then pour the sauce over the mushrooms, fish and spinach. Sprinkle with flaked almonds and bake in a medium oven at 350°F/180°C for about 20 minutes.

Serve with new potatoes and buttered carrots.

Friends were expected for supper, so I left the cooked chicken in the bath (the coolest place, before I acquired a refrigerator) and then went out.

My pet cat Toby, woken by the smell of something very tempting, went to investigate, and, after pushing open first the kitchen and then the bathroom doors discovered, to his utmost joy, the hidden treasure. Wasting not a minute, he jumped in beside it, and after making a small hole in the net cover just big enough to get his head through, commenced his sumptuous feast, keeping in mind that it would be extremely nice to come back for second helpings, and so only eating precisely half. Satisfied, and almost too fat to move, he made his way back to the kitchen, curled up on his favourite cushion and was soon fast asleep.

On my return home, one glimpse at the open doors and at Toby, by this time awake and looking exceedingly guilty, told me all. I was very cross, but couldn't resist a secret smile at his sheer craftiness.

He did not get the other half of his treasure, and in the end my guests dined off quickly defrosted chicken pieces supplied by my kind neighbour who came to the rescue!

CHICKEN PIE WITH FRESH TARRAGON AND WHITE WINE SAUCE *(Serves 6)*

1 medium sized chicken
1 onion
4 cloves
1 carrot
1 bay leaf
6 peppercorns
Salt
300 ml (½ pint) dry white wine
300 ml (½ pint) water
A few sprigs fresh tarragon

For the pastry:
350 g (12 oz) plain flour
175 g (6 oz) lard
50 g (2 oz) butter
5 tbsp. cold water

For the sauce:
50 g (2 oz) butter
50 g (2 oz) flour
300 ml (½ pint) milk
2 tbsp. freshly chopped tarragon
Salt and freshly ground pepper
300 ml (½ pint) stock (liquid in which the chicken has been cooked)

Place the chicken in a large pan, add the peeled onion stuck with the cloves, the carrot peeled and diced, the bay leaf, peppercorns and salt. Pour over the wine and water and add the sprigs of tarragon. Cover the pan with a lid and simmer gently for 1–1¼ hours, or until the chicken is cooked. Meanwhile make the pastry as follows: sift the flour and salt into a bowl and rub in half the fats until the mixture resembles fine breadcrumbs. Cut the rest of the fat in with a knife until it looks like small peas, then add water until mixture just holds together. Cover and place in the refrigerator to rest.

Remove the chicken from the pan and leave to cool a little. Boil the stock rapidly until it is reduced by one third, then strain and skim off any surplus fat. Remove the flesh from the chicken, cut into neat pieces, then place these in a deep pie dish and keep warm.

For the sauce; melt the butter in a pan, stir in the flour, cook for a minute then slowly blend in the stock, the milk, salt and pepper and lastly the chopped tarragon.

Pour this over the chicken and cover with the pastry that has been rolled out to fit the size of the dish. Flute the edges and make a small hole in the centre to let the steam escape. (A pie crock is a help to prevent the pastry from sinking whilst cooking.) Decorate the pie with pastry leaves and brush with beaten egg or milk. Bake in a pre-heated oven 400°F/200°C for about 30 minutes.

VEGETABLE CURRY WITH YOGHURT (*Serves 4*)

3 tbsp. sunflower oil
1 medium onion
1 clove garlic
1 tsp. turmeric
1 tsp. salt
1 tsp. garam masala
1 tsp. cardamoms
A pinch chilli
1 tsp. fresh or ½ tsp. dried coriander

225 g (½ lb) potatoes
3 good-sized carrots
1 small turnip
2 parsnips
3 sticks celery
1 small cauliflower or 225 g (½ lb) Brussels sprouts
1 400g (14oz) tin tomatoes
150 ml (¼ pint) vegetable stock
Carton natural yoghurt

Heat the oil in a heavy pan, then add the onion (peeled and sliced), the garlic peeled and finely sliced, the turmeric, salt, garam masala, cardamoms, chilli and coriander. Sauté in the oil for 5 minutes, then add the peeled and diced potatoes, carrots, turnip, parsnips, celery and lastly the cauliflower divided into florets or the Brussels sprouts cut in half. Stir over the heat for a further 5 minutes, then add the tin of tomatoes and the vegetable stock. Cook until the potatoes are soft, then remove from the heat and pile into a warmed serving dish.

Put a good spoonful of yoghurt on each portion, or put the yoghurt into a bowl and serve separately with poppadoms and tomato chutney. (See page 49.)

LAMB CASSEROLE WITH VEGETABLES AND DUMPLINGS (*Serves 4*)

1.4 kg (3 lbs) middle neck of lamb
50 g (2 oz) wholemeal flour
25 g (1 oz) dripping
2 onions
4 carrots
1 small turnip
2 parsnips
2 leeks
1 dsp. fresh or 1 tsp. dried rosemary
Salt and freshly ground black pepper
1 bay leaf

For the dumplings:
50 g (2 oz) self raising wholemeal flour
1 tsp. fresh or ½ tsp. dried mixed herbs
25 g (1 oz) shredded suet
Salt and freshly ground black pepper

Cut the meat from the bones and set aside. Place the bones in a saucepan, cover them with cold water and bring to the boil. Simmer for 30 minutes and remove any scum.

Meanwhile cut the meat into small pieces, coat with seasoned flour and quickly brown in a pan with the dripping. Then remove the meat with a slotted spoon and keep warm. Peel, dice or slice all the vegetables and mix together in a bowl with the rosemary, the salt and the freshly ground black pepper. Then, arrange layers of the meat and seasoned vegetables in a casserole, beginning and ending with a layer of vegetables. Strain the liquid from the bones, pour it over the casserole until it just reaches the top, add the bay leaf, and then place the casserole in the centre of a pre-heated oven, 350°F / 180°C for 2-2½ hours.

To make the dumplings, sift the flour into a small bowl and add the herbs, the suet and salt and pepper. Add enough water to make a soft dough, and divide this into four portions. Then, 30 minutes before the casserole is ready, place the dumplings on top of the meat and vegetables, cover with the lid and return the casserole to the oven until the cooking time is complete.

The gravy may be thickened with a little cornflour and water before adding the dumplings – if required.

LAMB WITH YOGHURT AND NASTURTIUM SEEDS *(Serves 4)*

Fortunately, nasturtiums grow very well in my garden, being one of those accommodating plants that flourish in almost any soil. They can be particularly effective when trailing in or around rows of vegetables. It is advisable to pickle the seeds in brine for six months before using them in this dish.

675 g (1 ½ lb) lean lamb (the leg is best)
25 g (1 oz) butter
1 tbsp. oil
1 large onion
1 clove garlic
25 g (1 oz) flour
300 ml (½ pint) vegetable stock
1 tbsp. pickled nasturtium seeds (or capers will do)
2 pickled dill cucumbers
Grated rind 1 lemon
1 tbsp. chopped parsley
300 ml (½ pint) natural yoghurt
Salt and freshly ground pepper

Cut the lamb into 2.5 cm (1 inch) cubes. Heat the butter and oil in a large pan and add the meat to seal on all sides. Transfer to a casserole and keep warm.

Peel and slice the onion and finely chop the garlic, then add to the juices in the pan and cook for about 5 minutes. Stir in the flour, cook for 1 minute, then add the stock and bring to the boil, stirring all the time. Season with salt and pepper and add the nasturtium seeds, dill cucumbers, lemon rind and parsley. Pour over the meat in the casserole and place in a pre-heated oven, 350°F / 160°C, for 1–1½ hours.

Just before serving, add the yoghurt and adjust the seasoning to taste. (Make sure not to let the sauce boil after you have added the yoghurt or it will curdle.)

CABBAGE, SAUSAGE AND TOMATO LAYER (*Serves* 4)

Outside leaves of a good, dark-green cabbage
450 g (1 lb) sausages (home-made if possible)
225 g (8 oz) mature cheddar cheese
25 g (1 oz) butter
1 large onion
1 clove garlic
25 g (1 oz) wholemeal flour
1 400 g (14 oz) tin peeled tomatoes
1 dsp. fresh or 1 tsp. dried oregano
Salt and freshly ground pepper
Brown breadcrumbs

Cook the cabbage leaves whole in a little boiling, salted water until just tender. Then, strain and keep them warm. Grill the sausages, cool them a little and slice into rounds. Grate the cheese.

Melt the butter in a saucepan and add the onion (peeled and sliced) and the garlic (crushed). Sauté them together for a few minutes, then add the flour, the tin of tomatoes – which have been puréed – the oregano and salt and pepper. Simmer gently until smooth and thick. Then put a layer of cabbage at the bottom of a buttered casserole, followed by half the sausages, some grated cheese and half the tomato sauce. Repeat this sequence finishing with a layer of cheese and breadcrumbs. Brown under the grill for about 15 minutes or until golden and bubbling hot.

Serve with a baked jacket potato.

SPINACH TIMBALE WITH TOMATO SAUCE *(Serves 4)*

4 eggs
300 ml (½ pint) milk
450 g (1 lb) fresh spinach, cooked and chopped
50 g (2 oz) wholemeal breadcrumbs
50 g (2 oz) mature cheddar cheese
½ tsp. freshly ground nutmeg
Salt and freshly ground pepper

For the sauce:
2 tbsp. oil
1 small onion
1 clove garlic
1 400 g (14 oz) tin tomatoes
1 tbsp. tomato purée
1-2 tsp. sugar
Salt and freshly ground pepper
1 tsp. fresh chopped or ½ tsp. dried basil

Beat the eggs and milk together in a bowl. Then stir in the chopped spinach, breadcrumbs, grated cheese, nutmeg and salt and pepper. Pour into a greased 1.1 L (2 pint) ovenproof dish or ring mould and then bake in a pre-heated oven at 350°F / 180°C for about 1 hour until set and slightly risen. Test with a skewer, which should come out clean. Serve straight from the dish or leave for a few minutes before turning out.

To make the sauce; heat the oil in a saucepan and sauté the peeled and finley chopped onion until just soft. Add the crushed garlic and cook for 1 minute. Then add the tomatoes, tomato purée, sugar and salt and pepper to taste. Bring to the boil, add the basil, cover and then simmer for 40 minutes. Liquidise for a smoother sauce and serve with the Timbale in a separate bowl.

SPINACH COULIBIAC *(Serves 5-6)*

225 g (½ lb) carrots
1 large onion
75 g (3 oz) butter (plus extra for flavouring)
1 tbsp. oil
225 g (8 oz) cream cheese
Salt and freshly ground pepper
1 medium turnip
1 potato
450 g (1 lb) fresh spinach
¼ tsp. freshly grated nutmeg
1 clove garlic
225 g (½ lb) mushrooms
225 g (8 oz) home-made flaky pastry or packet puff pastry

Peel and grate the carrots and finely slice the onion. Heat 25 g (1 oz) of the butter with the oil in a saucepan, gently fry the carrot and onion until soft, but not brown, then remove from the heat and stir in the cream cheese. Season well with salt and pepper.

Now peel and dice the turnip and potato, and cook them together in a saucepan of salted, boiling water. Then, remove from the heat and mash with butter, salt and pepper. Wash and roughly cut the spinach and cook in a little boiling, salted water until tender. Remove from the heat, and add a knob of butter, the freshly grated nutmeg and the garlic (crushed). Lastly, sauté the mushrooms in the remaining 50 g (2 oz) of butter.

Roll out the pastry to form a rectangle approximately 35 × 32 ½ cm/ 14 × 13 in. Arrange down the centre a layer of the turnips and potato, one of the spinach, one of the carrot mixture and finally one of the sautéed mushrooms then reverse this finishing with a layer of turnip and potato. Dampen the edges of the pastry with cold water and bring first together the two longest sides, sealing well, and then the two shorter ends, like you would when making a pasty or parcel. Brush the whole liberally with a beaten egg, and carefully place it on a greased baking sheet. Bake in a hot oven at 400°F/200°C for 30-40 minutes, or until golden brown and crispy.

This dish can either be eaten the way it is or served with tomato sauce. (See recipe for Spinach Timbale page 24.)

SPINACH QUICHE (*Serves 4*)

225 g (8 oz) shortcrust pastry
225 g (½ lb) freshly picked spinach
25 g (1 oz) butter
100 g (4 oz) cottage cheese
4 tbsp. single cream
2 eggs
Salt and freshly ground pepper
¼ tsp. freshly ground nutmeg
50 g (2 oz) Parmesan or cheddar cheese

Line a 20 cm (8 inch) flan dish with the pastry and bake blind in a pre-heated oven at 400°F / 200°C for 15 minutes remembering to remove the covering for the last 5 minutes.

Meanwhile, cook the spinach in a little salted water and drain it well to ensure all the moisture is removed. Toss in the butter and cut up roughly. Then, mix in the cottage cheese, cream, beaten eggs, salt, pepper and nutmeg to taste. Turn into the flan case, smooth the top and sprinkle with the grated cheese. Bake in a pre-heated oven at 350°F / 180°C for about 30 minutes.

Can be served hot or cold with a tossed salad.

SPINACH CRUMBLE (*Serves 4*)

225 g (½ lb) potatoes
1 small onion
450 g (1 lb) freshly picked spinach
225 g (8 oz) cheddar cheese
Salt and freshly ground pepper
¼ tsp. ground mace

For the crumble:
75 g (3 oz) butter
50 g (2 oz) wheatgerm
50 g (2 oz) wholemeal plain flour
50 g (2 oz) rolled oats and bran

Peel and dice the potatoes, cook with the sliced onion in a little salted water until soft, then drain and mash well. Then put the spinach into a small amount of boiling, salted water, cook until just tender and then drain, squeezing out all the excess water. Combine the mashed potatoes and onion, spinach, grated cheese, salt and pepper and mace, and place in a buttered casserole dish.

For the crumble, melt the butter in a frying pan, add the wheatgerm, wholemeal flour, rolled oats and bran, and mix them together well for 5 minutes. Place on top of the spinach mixture, and bake in a pre-heated oven at 400°F / 200°C for 30 minutes or until golden-brown and crunchy.

SPINACH, MUSHROOM AND WALNUT ROULADE *(Serves 6)*

450g (1lb) freshly picked spinach
Knob of butter
4 eggs
Salt and freshly ground pepper
25g (1oz) grated parmesan cheese

For the filling:
25g (1oz) butter
25g (1oz) wholemeal flour
150g (6oz) mushrooms
¼ pt milk
Pinch of nutmeg
50g (2oz) walnuts
1 tbsp. oil
¼ tsp. salt

Line a 30 × 20 cm/12" × 8" swiss roll tin with siliconised paper. Cook spinach in a little boiling salted water, drain well then add the knob of butter, chop well and place in a large bowl. Separate the eggs, add the yolks to the spinach, mix well and season with salt and freshly ground pepper. In a separate bowl whisk the egg whites until stiff then with a metal spoon quickly fold them into the spinach mixture. Turn into prepared tin, sprinkle parmesan cheese over the surface and bake in a pre-heated oven 400°F/200°C for 20 minutes. In the meantime make the filling as follows: heat the butter in a saucepan, slice mushrooms and sauté gently for about 5 minutes. Stir in the flour and cook for a minute, then slowly add the milk stirring all the time until sauce thickens and boils. Add the nutmeg and season to taste with salt and pepper. In a small saucepan heat the oil and add the walnuts which have been roughly chopped and the salt. Toss together for about 5 minutes, remove from the heat and with a slotted spoon add the walnuts to the mushroom mixture.

When the roulade is cooked remove from the oven, cover with a sheet of greaseproof paper and a damp teatowel for ½ hour, then turn out and spread with the mushroom and walnut filling and gently roll the roulade up.

Serve immediately.

SWEET-SOUR STUFFED CABBAGE LEAVES *(Serves 4–6)*

6 large cabbage leaves
2 tbsp. oil
100 g (4 oz) long-grain brown rice
1 bay leaf
1 medium onion
100 g (4 oz) mushrooms
A few slices streaky bacon
1 small red pepper
1 dsp. freshly chopped or 1 tsp. dried herbs
Salt and freshly ground pepper

For the sauce:
1 small onion
1 clove garlic
2 tbsp. oil
1 400 g (14 oz) tin tomatoes
1 carrot
2 tbsp. wine vinegar
50 g (2 oz) sultanas
2 tbsp. soya sauce

Blanch the cabbage leaves in boiling water, then drain and plunge into cold water.

Put 1 tbsp. oil into a saucepan. When it is hot, put in the rice, stir well until the grains are well coated, then add 300 ml (½ pint) of boiling water, the bay leaf and a pinch of salt. Cover and cook gently for 20 minutes or until all liquid is absorbed and the rice is soft.

Peel, slice and fry the onions in the remaining oil, adding the sliced mushrooms, the chopped bacon and red pepper which has been deseeded and sliced. Sprinkle in the herbs and continue cooking for 5 minutes. Then stir in the rice (removing the bay leaf) and mix everything well together; season to taste. Lay the cabbage leaves flat, spoon the rice mixture down the centre, then roll up and place side by side on a buttered, ovenproof dish.

For the sauce, sauté the sliced onion and finely sliced garlic in the oil, then add all the other ingredients and simmer for 15 minutes or until the sauce is thickened. Check the seasoning, then pour the sauce over the cabbage rolls, cover with a lid and place in a pre-heated oven at 350°F / 180°C for 30 minutes.

LEEKS WITH HAM AND CHEESE SAUCE (*Serves 4*)

4 good sized leeks
50 g (2 oz) butter
50 g (2 oz) wholemeal flour
600 ml (1 pint) milk
Salt and freshly ground pepper
½ tsp. ready-made mustard
100 g (4 oz) mature cheddar cheese
4 slices cooked ham (not too thin)

Wash the leeks well, trim the dark-green leaves and place the leeks in a saucepan of boiling, salted water. Cook until tender, then drain well.

Meanwhile, melt the butter in another saucepan, add the flour and stir together for a few minutes until smooth. Gradually add the milk, and continue stirring until the sauce thickens and boils. Then, add the salt and pepper, mustard and grated cheese.

Roll up each leek in a slice of ham, place them in a buttered, oven-proof dish, pour over the cheese sauce and then sprinkle generously with breadcrumbs which have been mixed with a little more of the grated cheese. Bake in a pre-heated oven at 350°F / 180°C for 20 minutes, or until golden brown.

This makes a good supper dish served with toast or a baked jacket potato.

BROAD BEAN CASSEROLE (*Serves 4*)

1.8 kg (4 lbs) broad beans
(weighed before shelling)
225 g (½ lb) stewing steak
225 g (½ b) Italian salami
4 rashers bacon
2 carrots
1 large onion
2 young turnips
4 tomatoes (or 1 400g (14oz) tin of tomatoes)
1 clove garlic
300 ml (½ pint) beef stock
Salt and freshly ground pepper
1 tbsp. fresh chopped herbs or 1 tsp. dried herbs

Firstly, shell the broad beans, trim and cube the steak, slice the salami and chop the bacon. Then fry the bacon gently and add the salami and meat. When brown, remove them from the pan and place in a casserole with the peeled and sliced carrots, onion, turnip (cut in small pieces), and the tomatoes and garlic which has been peeled and finely chopped. Cover them with the stock, season with salt and pepper and add the herbs. Place the lid on the casserole and cook in a pre-heated oven at 300°F / 150°C for 2 hours.

If preferred, the gravy can be thickened with a little cornflour mixed to a paste with cold water, 5 minutes before serving.

Baked jacket potatoes and any green vegetable go well with this.

I never thought I could grow onions until a relative of my neighbours gave me a magic set, and the successful results added a real touch of professionalism to the garden.

Here is one of my favourite recipes for using them:

ONION AND CHEESE FLAN (*Serves 4*)

100 g (4 oz) wholemeal flour
25 g (1 oz) lard
25 g (1 oz) butter
3 tbsp. water
1 tbsp. cooking oil
1 tsp. brown sugar

For the filling:
330 g (¾ lb) onions
50 g (2 oz) butter
2 eggs
2 tbsp. double cream
75 g (3 oz) mature cheddar cheese
Salt and freshly ground pepper
A little freshly grated nutmeg

Put the flour into a bowl, and rub in the lard and 25 g (1 oz) of the butter until it resembles fine breadcrumbs. Add the water and oil, together with the sugar, and leave in a cool place for half an hour.

Meanwhile prepare the filling, peel and chop the onions and sauté in the butter until transparent but not brown. Then, place the eggs in a bowl, beat them well and add the cream, grated cheese, salt, pepper and nutmeg. Lastly, add the cooked onions. Roll out the pastry to cover a 20 cm (8 inch) flan tin, and pour in the onion mixture. Bake in a pre-heated oven at 400°F/200°C for 20 minutes.

COUNTRY VEGETABLE PIE (*Serves 4*)

2 leeks
4 carrots
4 young turnips (or one small swede)
50 g (2 oz) butter
50 g (2 oz) wholemeal flour
600 ml (1 pint) milk
Salt and freshly ground pepper
¼ tsp. ground mace
1 tbsp. fresh chopped parsley
100 g (4 oz) cubed, cooked ham (optional)
225 g (8 oz) home-made flaky pastry or packet puff pastry

Wash the leeks, and cut them into 5 cm (2 inch) lengths. Peel and slice the carrots, scrub the turnips and cut both into quarters (if using swede, peel and cut into similar-sized pieces). Put them all into a saucepan of boiling, salted water and cook until just tender. Drain well and set aside.

Melt the butter in another saucepan, add the flour and cook gently for 1 minute. Then, gradually add the milk, stirring all the time until the sauce thickens and boils. Add the salt, pepper, mace and chopped parsley, and, lastly, the cubed cooked ham and all the vegetables, then pour into a pie dish. Set a pie crock in the centre and cover over with the pastry, rolled out to a 0.5 cm (¼ inch) thickness. Brush the surface with beaten egg and bake in a pre-heated oven at 400°F/200°C for 20-30 minutes.

According to the time of year, different vegetables can be used. Celeriac is good, and so are artichokes and parsnips.

OVEN SLICED POTATOES WITH CHEESE AND HERBS *(Serves 6)*

4-6 good-sized potatoes
2 medium onions
Butter
Salt and freshly ground pepper
100 g (4 oz) cheddar cheese
2-3 dsp. fresh or 2-3 tsp. dried herbs
Milk

Peel and finely slice the potatoes and the onions. Butter an ovenproof dish, and arrange successive layers of potatoes, onions and grated cheese, with a sprinkling of the herbs, salt and pepper and several knobs of butter. Pour over sufficient milk to come halfway up the sides of the dish and then bake in a pre-heated oven at 350°F/180°C for about one hour, or until the potatoes are soft and golden-brown on top.

This recipe for a traditional Swiss breakfast was given to me by a friend from Basel who came to stay on holiday.

RÖSCHTÉ *(Serves 4)*

450 g (1 lb) potatoes
5-6 slices streaky bacon
1 small onion
Salt and freshly ground pepper
Butter or bacon fat, for frying

Boil the potatoes in their skins until just cooked and allow them to get cold. Then, remove the skins and coarsely grate. Chop and lightly fry the bacon together with the peeled and finely sliced onion, then season with salt and pepper and mix together with the potatoes. Put the butter or bacon fat into a large, heavy frying pan, heat until bubbling, then add the bacon and potato mixture, press it down well into a flat shape and cook for about 10 minutes on each side until golden and crusty.

Can be eaten with sausages, liver, or just a fried egg.

BEETROOT IN ORANGE SAUCE

6 medium beetroots
25 g (1 oz) butter
2 dsp. soft brown sugar
1 tsp. cornflour
1 orange and enough fresh orange juice to make up 300 ml (½ pint)
Salt and freshly ground pepper

Boil the beetroots in their skins until cooked (about 1 hour), peel, quarter and set aside.

Melt the butter in a saucepan together with the brown sugar, the grated rind and the juice of the orange and the extra orange juice (taking it up to 300 ml ½ pint). Stir over a low heat until the sugar has dissolved, then bring to the boil and add the cornflour (mixed with a little water), the salt and freshly ground pepper. Then, simmer for a few minutes before adding the beetroots. Cover the pan and leave to simmer gently until the beetroots are heated through and the sauce a rich red colour.

Put in a bowl and serve sprinkled with fresh, chopped parsley.

TURNIP AND PEAR BAKE

(Serves 4)

6 medium or 10 small turnips
2 fresh pears
300 ml (½ pint) single cream
Salt and freshly ground pepper
¼ tsp. freshly grated nutmeg

Layer the diced turnips and sliced pears in a buttered, oven-proof dish. Pour over the cream, season with salt, pepper and nutmeg, and cover with a lid. Bake in a pre-heated oven at 350°F/180°C for about three quarters of an hour or until soft.

(Sliced onions can also be added to this dish.)

LEMON-GLAZED CARROTS *(Serves 6)*

1 kg (2 lbs) carrots
300 ml (½ pint) boiling water
1 chicken stock cube
2 tbsp. soft brown sugar
50 g (2 oz) butter
Salt and freshly ground pepper
Juice ½ a lemon
¼ tsp. freshly ground nutmeg
2 tbsp. chopped parsley

Cut the carrots into thin strips and place them in boiling, salted water together with the stock cube, brown sugar, butter, salt and pepper. Cover and simmer until the carrots are tender, then remove them with a slotted spoon and keep warm. Thicken the liquid in the pan with a little cornflour mixed with water, add the lemon juice, nutmeg and chopped parsley, then pour over the carrots and serve in a warmed dish.

CABBAGE WITH CUMIN SEEDS *(Serves 6)*

1 medium cabbage
1 small onion
50 g (2 oz) butter
1 tsp. cumin seeds
Salt and freshly ground pepper

Finely shred the cabbage and peel and slice the onion. Heat the butter in a large, heavy pan and, when bubbling, add the cabbage and onion. Sauté them together for a few minutes, then add the cumin seed, salt and pepper and enough water to prevent the contents sticking to the bottom of the pan. Cover tightly and simmer gently, giving a good shake now and again until the cabbage and onion are just cooked but still crispy. Serve immediately.

BROAD BEANS WITH POPPY SEEDS *(Serves 4)*

450 g (1 lb) broad beans
(after shells have been removed)
Sprig fresh mint
25 g (1 oz) butter
Salt and freshly ground pepper
2 tsp. poppy seeds

Put the broad beans into a saucepan of boiling, salted water with the sprig of mint. Cook until tender, then drain well, remove the mint and add the butter, giving another good shake to the pan. Season with salt and pepper and add the poppy seeds. Shake again and serve in a warmed dish.

SPICY RED CABBAGE

450 g (1 lb) red cabbage
1 large onion
1 large cooking apple
25 g (1 oz) butter
¼ tsp. ground cloves
2 tbsp. water
2 tbsp. vinegar (cider or wine)
1 tsp. salt
½ tsp. ground cumin
1 tbsp. soft brown sugar
Salt and freshly ground black pepper

Finely slice the cabbage, and peel and slice both the onion and the apple. Melt the butter in a large saucepan and add all the other ingredients. Cover with a tight-fitting lid and simmer for 1 hour, or until the cabbage is tender. Stir occasionally to prevent it from burning and add a little more water if necessary; by the time it is cooked there should be hardly any liquid left in the pan.

COLESLAW WITH SALTED PEANUTS

Finely slice some cabbage and mix this together with some grated carrot and apple, a good handful of raisins, some chopped spring onions, freshly ground pepper and another good handful of salted peanuts. Mix them together well, with enough mayonnaise to knit the whole together, then turn out into a serving bowl and sprinkle with chopped parsley.

SPINACH WITH PINE KERNELS AND MUSHROOMS

225 g (½ lb) freshly picked spinach
100 g (4 oz) mushrooms
4 spring onions
50 g (2 oz) pine kernels (toasted)

For the dressing:
1 tbsp. wine vinegar
1 tsp. sugar
2 tbsp. sunflower oil
¼ tsp. mustard
1 tbsp. olive oil
Freshly ground pepper and a pinch salt

Finely slice the spinach, mushrooms and spring onions and add the pine kernels. Put all the dressing ingredients into a screw-top jar and shake well. Pour over the salad and mix thoroughly. If you like garlic, add 1 small clove (crushed).

LETTUCE, ORANGE AND WALNUT SALAD

1 medium-sized lettuce
2 oranges
4 spring onions
Cucumber
A few radishes
50 g (2 oz) chopped walnuts

For the dressing:
150 ml (¼ pint) natural yoghurt
½ tsp. celery seeds
Lemon juice
1 tsp. light brown sugar
Salt and freshly ground pepper

Shred the lettuce, then peel the orange and divide it into segments. Finely slice the spring onions, dice the cucumber and radishes, then mix all these up in a bowl together with the chopped walnuts. Mix all the dressing ingredients together adding a little milk if the consistency is too thick, and then pour them over the salad and toss well.

CARROT, LEMON AND WATERCRESS SALAD

225 g (½ lb) carrots
1 tbsp. soft brown sugar
Juice 1 lemon
Freshly ground pepper
A good handful watercress

Grate the carrots, sprinkle over the brown sugar, then add the lemon juice and mix together well. Season with the freshly ground pepper to taste, and leave for 20 minutes for the liquids to be absorbed.

Just before serving, combine all with the watercress and pile into a serving dish.

RHUBARB AND ORANGE CRUMBLE *(Serves 4)*

450 g (1 lb) rhubarb
3 tbsp. soft brown sugar
1 orange

For the crumble:
75 g (3 oz) butter
50 g (2 oz) soft brown sugar
75 g (3 oz) wholemeal flour
50 g (2 oz) oat flakes
25 g (1 oz) oatmeal
1 tsp. mixed spice

Cut up the rhubarb and place in a saucepan with the sugar, the grated rind of the orange and the juice to which 2 tbsp. water has been added. Gently cook over a low heat until the rhubarb is soft. Cool slightly, and place in an oven proof dish.

To make the crumble, cream the butter and the sugar together until light and fluffy, then add the flour, oat flakes, oatmeal and mixed spice. Mix lightly together and sprinkle over the top of the rhubarb. Place in a pre-heated oven at 375°F / 190°C and bake for 20 minutes or until golden-brown.

Serve with custard or whipped cream.

RHUBARB AND GINGER FOOL *(Serves 6)*

450 g (1 lb) rhubarb
3 tbsp. light brown sugar
2.5 cm (1 inch) piece fresh ginger or
½ tsp. ground ginger
300 ml (½ pint) ready-made custard
150 ml (¼ pint) double cream
1 egg white (optional)

Cut up the rhubarb and place in a saucepan together with the sugar, a little water and the piece of root ginger, which has been bruised and put inside a muslin bag, alternatively add the ground ginger. Simmer gently until the rhubarb is cooked, remove the muslin bag, cool a little and then liquidise. Then make the custard and whip the cream, and add both to the rhubarb, folding in carefully. Lastly, whisk the egg white, and fold this in too. Pour into a serving bowl and place in the refrigerator for 1-2 hours.

Sprinkle with a few chopped nuts before placing on the table.

RHUBARB AND FIG PIE *(Serves 5)*

450 g (1 lb) rhubarb
100 g (4 oz) dried figs
3 tbsp. soft brown sugar
3 tbsp. water
175 g (6 oz) plain flour
¼ tsp. salt
75 g (3 oz) lard
25 g (1 oz) margarine
½ tsp. sugar
3 tbsp. cold water

Cut up the rhubarb and place in a saucepan with the figs (roughly chopped), the sugar and the 3 tbsp. water. Simmer gently until the rhubarb is cooked, then thicken with a little cornflour mixed with water. Remove from the heat and cool completely.

Sift the flour and salt into a bowl and rub in half the fats until the mixture resembles fine breadcrumbs. Cut in the rest of the fat with a knife, to look like small peas, then add the sugar and sufficient water so that the mixture just holds together.

Roll this out onto a floured board, line a 20 cm (8 inch) tin with half the pastry, and then pour in the rhubarb mixture and cover with the remaining pastry, making sure to dampen the edges to seal well together. Brush the pie with milk and sprinkle generously with demerara sugar. Bake in a pre-heated oven at 400°F/200°C for 20 minutes or until golden-brown. Serve with whipped cream .

Gooseberries or blackcurrants can be used as an alternative filling.

GOOSEBERRY AND ELDERFLOWER PANCAKES *(Serves 6)*

For the pancakes:
100 g (4 oz) plain flour
Pinch of salt
2 eggs
300 ml (½ pint) milk
1 tbsp. melted butter

For the filling:
450 g (1 lb) gooseberries
One handful elderflowers
6 tbsp. white wine
2 tbsp. honey

To make the pancakes, sift the flour and salt into a bowl and make a well in the centre. Beat together the eggs and milk, and add these gradually to the flour with the melted butter. Beat until the batter becomes smooth, then cover with a cloth and leave to stand for 1 hour.

To make the filling, put the gooseberries into a saucepan with the elderflowers and the white wine. Cook over a low heat until soft, then pass through a sieve and, whilst still hot, stir in the honey. Keep them warm.

To assemble the pancakes, lightly oil a small heavy frying pan and heat well. Stir the batter well, then add about 2 tbsp. to the pan, tilting immediately so that the batter coats the base evenly. Brown lightly on one side, then turn and brown the other. Transfer it to a warm plate, cover with a sheet of greaseproof paper and place it over a pan of simmering water. Continue making pancakes until all the batter is used up.

Spoon a little of the warm gooseberry and elderflower mixture down the centre of each pancake, then roll up carefully. Dust with icing sugar and serve with whipped cream.

GOOSEBERRY AND ELDERFLOWER MOUSSE *(Serves 6)*

450 g (1 lb) gooseberries
300 ml (½ pint) elderflowers
150 g (6 oz) caster sugar
3 large eggs
15 g (½ oz) gelatine
300 ml (½ pint) double cream

Put the gooseberries and elderflowers in a saucepan, then add 75 g (3 oz) of the sugar and 150 ml (¼ pint) of water. Place over a gentle heat and simmer until the gooseberries are soft. Draw the pan from the heat, cool a little, remove any elderflower stalks and then liquidise. Separate the eggs. Put the yolks in a bowl with the remaining 75 g (3 oz) of sugar, beat well until thick and pale and add this to the puréed gooseberries and elderflowers. Place 3 tbsp. cold water in a cup, sprinkle over the gelatine, leave for a few minutes, for it to turn spongy, and then place in a pan of simmering water until all the granules have dissolved. Pour this into the gooseberry and elderflower mixture, then whip the cream, fold this in, then whisk the egg whites until very stiff and fold these in lastly. When completely smooth, pour into a serving bowl and place in the refrigerator for 1-2 hours.

Serve with a finger of shortbread (see page 135).

BLACKCURRANT CHARLOTTE *(Serves 4-6)*

450-675 g (1-1 ½ lbs) blackcurrants
100 g (4 oz) caster sugar
175-225 g (6-8 oz) wholemeal breadcrumbs
50 g (2 oz) soft brown sugar
75 g (3 oz) suet
Grated rind 1 lemon

Place the blackcurrants in a saucepan with the caster sugar and very little water, and simmer gently until cooked.

Mix the breadcrumbs, soft brown sugar, suet and lemon rind together and press a thin layer onto the base of a greased ovenproof dish. Put this into a pre-heated oven, 375°F/190°C, and leave for about 10 minutes. Then, remove the dish and fill it with alternate layers of fruit and crumbs, finishing with a layer of crumbs. Return it to the oven, reduce the heat to 350°F/180°C and cook for half an hour until rich brown in colour. Serve with whipped cream.

SUMMER PUDDING (*Serves 6*)

Line a wetted pudding-basin with slices of day-old white bread. Put approximately 500 g (1 lb) blackcurrants and redcurrants mixed together into a saucepan with 100 g (4 oz) sugar and 75 ml (⅛ pint) water. Simmer gently until soft then pour into the prepared basin and cover the top with more slices of bread and finally with a saucer topped with a weight. Leave in a cool place for several hours (overnight if possible), then turn out onto a serving plate, cut into slices and serve with whipped cream.

Any juices that are left over can be thickened with arrowroot and made into a sauce.

BLACKCURRANT & MINT SORBET (*Serves 4*)

500 g (1 lb) blackcurrants
300 ml (½ pint) water
A few sprigs applemint (or any mint will do)
2 tsps. powdered gelatine
150 g (8 oz) caster sugar
2 egg whites

Put the blackcurrants into a saucepan with the mint leaves and cook gently until the currants are soft. Cool a little then liquidise and pass through a sieve to remove the pips. Place the gelatine over a pan of hot water and and when it dissolves pour this onto the fruit mixture and blend well. Pour into a freezer container and freeze uncovered for about 2 hours, or until ice begins to form around the edges of the container. Turn out into a bowl, whisk the egg whites until stiff and fold into the sorbet. Return to the container, cover and freeze until required.

Arrange small scoops of the sorbet in serving glasses, and decorate with mint leaves.

UPSIDE-DOWN BLACKCURRANT PUDDING *(Serves 4)*

450 g (1 lb) blackcurrants
50 g (2 oz) granulated sugar
75 g (3 oz) self raising flour
A pinch of salt
50 g (2 oz) shredded suet
25 g (1 oz) butter
25 g (1 oz) soft brown sugar
1 tsp. arrowroot

Place the blackcurrants in a saucepan with the granulated sugar and 150 ml (¼ pint) water. Simmer gently until cooked then strain and reserve the liquid.

Brush a 600 ml (1 pint) pudding-basin with some melted butter. Then sift the flour and salt into a bowl, add the suet and mix to a soft dropping consistency with 3-4 tbsp. of the reserved liquid. Cream the butter and brown sugar together until light and fluffy and spread evenly over the base of the greased pudding-basin. Then, add the drained blackcurrants and, finally, the suet mixture smoothing with a knife. Cover with a double layer of buttered foil and steam for 1 ½ hours in a saucepan of simmering water coming halfway up the sides of the bowl.

Turn the pudding out on to a warmed plate and serve with the remaining blackcurrant juice thickened with the arrowroot which has been mixed with a little cold water before adding to the liquid.

STRAWBERRY AND MERINGUE SHORTCAKE *(Serves 4)*

For the base:
100 g (4 oz) butter
140 g (5 oz) plain flour
25 g (1 oz) cornflour
50 g (2 oz) caster sugar

For the topping:
450 g (1 lb) fresh strawberries
2 egg whites
50 g (2 oz) caster sugar

Rub the butter into the flour and cornflour until it resembles fine breadcrumbs. Add the sugar and keep on kneading until it forms a dough. Roll out on a floured surface then shape into either an oblong or a circle, and place on a baking sheet. Bake in a pre-heated oven, 350°F/180°C, for 1 hour or until golden-brown.

When the shortcake has cooled, liberally cover with the strawberries, which have been halved or quartered. Then whisk the egg whites and, when stiff, add the sugar one spoonful at a time, whisking well between each addition. Cover the strawberries with the meringue and bake in a pre-heated oven, 400°F/200°C, for 10 minutes. Decorate with strawberry halves and serve with single cream.

STRAWBERRY AND ORANGE PAVLOVA *(Serves 6)*

4 egg whites (2-3 days old are best)
100 g (4 oz) caster sugar
100 g (4 oz) icing sugar
1 tsp. wine vinegar
300 ml (½ pint) double cream
Grated rind 2 oranges
450 g (1 lb) strawberries

Line a baking tray with a sheet of non-stick parchment. Put the egg whites into a bowl and, with a balloon or hand whisk, whisk them until stiff, add half the sugar a spoonful at a time, whisking between each addition, and then carefully fold in the remaining sugar with a metal spoon together with the vinegar. Pile the mixture on to the prepared baking tray, and shape it into a nest approximately 25 cm (10 inches) in diameter. Place in a cool oven, 200°F / 110°C, for 2-3 hours.

Then, remove the paper and set on a serving plate to get completely cold. Whip the cream, add the grated orange rind (a little Cointreau here is lovely for a special occasion), and spoon this into the hollowed-out part of the meringue. Finally, wash and halve (or quarter) the strawberries and place on the top. Refrigerate until ready to eat.

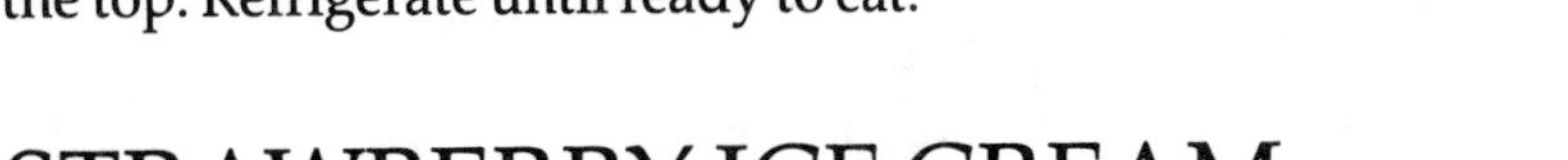

STRAWBERRY ICE CREAM *(Serves 6)*

450 g (1 lb) strawberries (less 6-8 for decoration)
3 eggs
75 g (3 oz) caster sugar
300 ml (½ pint) double cream

Wash and hull the strawberries, put them into a bowl and mash well. Then separate the eggs, whisk the yolks and the sugar together until thick and pale in colour, then carefully fold in the mashed strawberries. Whip the cream into soft peaks and fold this also into the strawberry mixture. Lastly, beat the egg whites until stiff and fold these in.

Place in a plastic container and put in the freezer for several hours. Remove half an hour before serving to soften a little, then scoop into individual glass bowls and decorate with a few extra strawberries.

Serve with a finger of shortbread. (See page 135.)

RHUBARB JAM WITH GINGER AND LEMON

Use equal amounts of rhubarb to sugar. This recipe is for 1.8 kg (4 lbs) of fruit.

Cut the rhubarb into small cubes, place in a bowl, cover with the sugar (soft brown and white, mixed) and leave to stand for 12 hours.

Then put a piece of root ginger (approx. 25 g 1 oz) in a muslin bag, bruise well and place in the preserving pan together with the rhubarb and sugar, and the juice of 2 lemons plus the grated rind of one. Bring to the boil slowly, making sure to stir occasionally to prevent the sugar from burning. Boil rapidly for about 20 minutes – or until a slight skin forms when a spoonful is put on a saucer and left to get cold. Finally, remove the muslin bag and pour into warmed jars, sealing in the normal way.

(Try using 225 g (8 oz) chopped figs, or 3 sticks of cinnamon, instead of the ginger.)

RHUBARB AND ORANGE JAM

2.7 kg (6 lbs) rhubarb
1.8 kg (4 lbs) sugar
2 oranges

Wash the rhubarb, cut into small pieces, place in a bowl with the sugar and leave for 12 hours.

Then, boil the oranges whole until just tender, remove any pips, slice finely and place in a preserving pan together with the rhubarb and sugar. Bring to the boil slowly, stirring occasionally until the sugar has dissolved. Boil rapidly for about 20 minutes – or until the jam sets when tested on a saucer – then pour into warmed jars and seal in the normal way.

GOOSEBERRY AND ELDERFLOWER JAM

2.7 kg (6 lbs) gooseberries
4 sprigs elderflowers (florets only)
1.1 L (2 pints) water
3.6 kg (8 lbs) sugar

Wash and top and tail the gooseberries. Place in a preserving pan with the elderflowers and the water and simmer gently for about 20 minutes or until the fruit is soft and mushy. Add the warmed sugar, dissolve slowly and then boil rapidly for 15 minutes or until the jam sets when tested on a saucer. Pour into warmed jars and seal in the normal way.

BLACKCURRANT AND APPLEMINT JAM

1.8 kg (4 lbs) blackcurrants
2 handfuls of applemint leaves
1.7 L (3 pints) water
2.7 kg (6 lbs) sugar

Remove the stems from the blackcurrants and place them in a preserving pan with the applemint leaves and the water. Bring to the boil and cook gently until the fruit is soft. Stir in the warmed sugar, keep stirring until it has dissolved and then boil rapidly for 15-20 minutes or until the jam sets when tested on a saucer. Draw the pan off the heat remove the mint leaves and then pour the jam into warmed jars and seal in the normal way.

STRAWBERRY JAM WITH LEMON

1.8 kg (4 lbs) strawberries
1.8 kg (4 lbs) sugar
Juice of 2 lemons

Wash, hull and drain the strawberries, layer with the sugar in a large bowl, then cover with a cloth and leave for 24 hours.

Put into a preserving pan with the juice from the lemons and bring slowly to the boil, stirring occasionally. Then, boil rapidly for about 20 minutes or until the jam sets when tested on a saucer. Remove from the heat and pour into warmed jars. Seal in the normal way.

STRAWBERRY JAM WITH GOOSEBERRIES

1.4 kg (3 lbs) strawberries
450 g (1 lb) gooseberries
225 ml (8 fl oz) water
1.8 kg (4 lbs) sugar

Wash and hull the strawberries and top and tail the gooseberries. Place the gooseberries in a preserving pan with the water and simmer gently until soft. Add the strawberries and continue simmering for a further 45 minutes. Add the warmed sugar – stir over a low heat until it is dissolved, then boil rapidly for 15-20 minutes or until the jam sets when tested on a saucer. Remove from the heat and pour into warmed jars. Seal in the normal way.

RHUBARB CHUTNEY

This recipe has been kindly donated by Mary McDonald of Edinbane.

450 g (1 lb) rhubarb
2 onions
2 tsp. curry powder
10 tbsp. cider vinegar
1 tsp. salt
Freshly ground pepper
2 tbsp. soft brown sugar

Wash and cube the rhubarb, finely slice the onions, then put in a preserving pan with the rest of the ingredients. Simmer gently until soft and then boil rapidly until fully cooked. Pour into warmed jars, and seal in the usual way.

(Variations: Add garlic and pickling spices, *or* less rhubarb and more onion.)

BEETROOT CHUTNEY

1.4 kg (3 lbs) raw beetroot
675 g (1 ½ lbs) cooking apples
2 large onions
225 g (8 oz) demerara sugar
600 ml (1 pint) cider or wine vinegar
1 level tsp. ground ginger, or
  2.5 cm (1 inch) grated root ginger
1 tsp. pickling spices
2 tsp. lemon juice
1 tbsp. salt

Boil the beetroot in a saucepan of salted water for about 2 hours or until cooked. Cool, remove the skins and chop into small cubes. Then, peel, core and chop the apples, and peel and finely slice the onions. Place all the ingredients in a preserving pan, bring slowly to the boil, stirring frequently, and simmer until soft and thick. Remove from the heat, and pour into warmed jars. Seal in the usual way.

Although I cannot successfully grow tomatoes without a greenhouse, sometimes I do get given some by friends, and if the weather has not blessed us with too much sunshine, the following recipe can be useful:

GREEN TOMATO CHUTNEY

1.4 kg (3 lbs) green tomatoes
 (or a mixture of green and red)
2 large onions
450 g (1 lb) eating apples
15 g (½ oz) root ginger
175 g (6 oz) sultanas
15 g (½ oz) salt
400 g (14 oz) dark brown sugar
600 ml (1 pint) cider or wine vinegar
½ tsp. crushed peppercorns

Chop the tomatoes, peel and chop the onions and apples. Bruise the ginger and put in a muslin bag. Put these and all the remaining ingredients into a preserving pan, bring slowly to the boil, stirring frequently, then simmer until the mixture is thick and soft. Remove the muslin bag and pour into warmed jars. Seal in the usual way.

Store for 2-3 months before using.

FROM THE SHORE

Gathering shellfish is one of the privileges enjoyed by those living close to the sea, and I often scold myself for not making better use of its valuable food source. The shore, no more than a few minutes' walk from my house, is easily reached for 'winkling', and is also a lovely place to take the dogs for a good romp on a fine day.

Over the years, the collecting of winkles (or *periwinkles* to give them their other name) has provided the local people with a valuable income. The small, snail-like creatures, anything up to an inch (2.5 cm) high, are a delicacy in French and Spanish restaurants, and although the demand may fluctuate according to the time of year, the market seems to remain constant, and it is seldom that the shore is seen at low tide (particularly in winter, when prices are at their highest) without at least two or three humped and hooded figures, backs to the wind, searching for their unsuspecting subjects to pop into a pail.

Winkles can come in a variety of colours but the most common ones are either black or brown. You can start looking for them from about half-tide level to the lowest ebb, and they are usually found under stones or large clumps of seaweed. Like us, they enjoy the warmth, and when conditions are favourable, love to sit out on the sand or rocks to sun themselves, inadvertently posing the ideal catch for busy hands! From the bucket stage, they are put into sacks, and, when the tide is completely over, they are taken home and placed at the roadside, ready for when the lorry comes to collect, weigh and pay us our hard-earned money, not forgetting to leave more bags for the next tide!

I have gathered winkles most winters since coming to Skye, so know what a hardship it can be when gale-force winds and lashing rain find a way through the toughest waterproofs, or when a sudden blizzard sweeping in from the Atlantic obliterates both bucket and winkles within seconds. Such moments are testing for the most stoic spirit, but then, in contrast, there come those perfect clear calm days when there is not a ripple on the water, and the plaintive cry of an oyster-catcher, or the soft cooings of the female eider duck with her young, lift the heart and make worthwhile all the hard work that has gone before. Anyway, enough of such reminiscences, and on with some more recipes.

There are not many ways of cooking winkles that I know of, but here are two. The first is the traditional method, while the second version is enhanced by a touch of garlic.

WINKLES COOKED THE TRADITIONAL WAY

Scrub the winkles clean, making sure to remove all the sand and grit. Put them into boiling, salted water for 5-10 minutes, strain and pile onto a serving plate. Eat with a pin.

For a slight variation, the winkles can be boiled in a *court-bouillon*, made from 0.5-1.1 L (1-2 pints) of water, one onion, one carrot – peeled and sliced – *bouquet-garni* and one clove of garlic.

WINKLES IN GARLIC BUTTER

Prepare the winkles as in the traditional method, using the *court-bouillon*. When cooked, remove them with a pin, divide equally into small, ovenproof bowls or ramekins and keep warm whilst making the garlic butter.

Take 100-225 g (¼ – ½ lb) butter, some chopped parsley and one or two cloves of crushed garlic, and put them all into a saucepan together with plenty of freshly ground pepper and a little salt. Place this over a gentle heat until the butter is melted and just beginning to bubble. Pour over the winkles, garnish with a little more chopped parsley and serve immediately with warm granary rolls. (See page 115.)

Another delicacy similar to the winkle but not so commonly found on the shores around Skye is the whelk, or 'buckie' as some Scots prefer to call them. These can be scrubbed and cleaned, boiled in salted water for 10-15 minutes and eaten with vinegar, or more popular is to cook them the way the French do snails in a *court-bouillon* and serve hot with French bread and plenty of good white wine.

WHELKS A LA BOURGUIGNONNE

Scrub and thoroughly clean the whelks and boil for 10-15 minutes in a *court-bouillon* (the same as for winkles). Let them cool and, meanwhile, work together in a small bowl 100-225 g (¼–½ lb) butter, 1-2 crushed cloves of garlic, some chopped parsley, plenty of freshly ground pepper and a little salt. Remove the whelks from their shells with a pin, wash the shells and put a small bit of the butter mixture at the bottom of each shell. Replace the whelks, and fill with more butter mixture. Then arrange the whelks on a baking dish, and place in a pre-heated oven, 400°F / 200°C, until bubbling hot.

Mussels are easy to find on most shores along the west coast, and grow quickly in dense masses. They are dark bluish-grey in colour and normally 5-7 cm (2-3 inches) long. The best time to go looking for them is at the low tide, when the rocks to which they cling are visible and the mussels can be easily removed.

Mussels need to be washed well before cooking. A scrubbing brush is useful for removing any growth from the shells, and it is important to discard any which are open, as these are either dead or diseased. Then, the best way to ensure that no grit or sand remains within the shell is to place them in a bucket of sea water (salted water will also do) to which a good handful of oatmeal has been added. The mussels will strain this through their filtration system and, in so doing, take away any impurities.

Probably one of the most popular and well known methods of preparing mussels is that simple and delicious dish *Moules Marinière*, so here is a recipe for this:

MOULES MARINIÈRE *(Serves 4)*

2 small onions
1 clove garlic
1 large wine glass dry white wine
1 large wine glass water
A sprig or two fresh thyme
Salt and freshly ground pepper
2-3 L (4-5 pints) mussels
50 g (2 oz) butter (cut into marbles and rolled in flour)
Chopped parsley

Peel and slice the onions and garlic, and place in a saucepan together with the white wine, water, thyme, salt and pepper. Bring to the boil and simmer gently until the liquid has reduced by one third. Then, add the mussels and bring back to the boil. Continue boiling for about 5 minutes or until the shells open. Transfer the mussels to a warmed serving bowl, then put the strained liquor into another saucepan and add to it the butter marbles and plenty of chopped parsley. When this has been allowed to cook for a little, pour over the mussels and serve with garlic bread. (See page 114.)

The following recipe was given to me by a friend from Switzerland who came to stay with me during the cold month of February. I was winkling, whilst she was gathering the mussels.

MUSSELS AS A SAVOURY *(Serves 3-4)*

25-30 mussels
1 onion
50 g (2 oz) butter
50 g (2 oz) flour
300 ml (½ pint) stock
150 ml (¼ pint) milk
1 tbsp. wine vinegar
1 tbsp. lemon juice
Salt and freshly ground pepper
2 sprigs parsley

Wash the mussels in the way already described, and place in a pan containing 600 ml (1 pint) of boiling water and half the onion (cut into quarters). Bring back to the boil, and, immediately the mussels open, remove from the heat and strain the liquid, reserve 300 ml (½ pint).

Melt the butter in a saucepan, add the other half of the onion (finely chopped) and sauté lightly until transparent but not brown. Stir in the flour, and blend together before adding the stock and milk. Continue stirring until the sauce thickens and bubbles, then add the vinegar, lemon juice, salt and pepper to taste, together with the chopped parsley and, lastly, the mussels, which have been removed from their shells and carefully separated from any pearls. Re-heat gently, and serve on a slice of buttered toast.

MOULES AU GRATIN *(Serves 4)*

2.3 L (4 pints) mussels
Wholemeal breadcrumbs
1 wine glass dry white wine
Chopped parsley
1 wine glass water
Grated parmesan cheese

Wash the mussels in the way already described. Put the wine and water in a large saucepan, bring to the boil and add the mussels together with a pinch of salt. Bring back to the boil and continue boiling until the shells open. Strain and reserve the liquor.

Arrange each mussel on a half-shell, and place closely together in a shallow, ovenproof dish. Cover liberally with the breadcrumbs, parsley and grated cheese, then pour over the strained liquor, adding a little more wine if liked, and place in a pre-heated oven 350°F / 180°C, for about 15 minutes.

Serve with garlic bread (see page 114).

MUSSEL CHOWDER (*Serves 6*)

2 doz mussels
600 ml (1 pt) water
150 ml (¼pt) dry white wine
1 bay leaf
Few sprigs parsley
2 sticks celery
2 onions
450 g (1 lb)potatoes
25 g (1 oz)butter
600 ml (1 pt) milk
Juice of ½ lemon
Salt and freshly ground pepper
25 g (1 oz) flour
Chopped parsley to garnish

Wash the mussels in the way already described and place in a large saucepan with the water, wine, bay leaf, parsley, celery sticks and one of the onions peeled and quartered. Bring to the boil and when the mussels open, remove from the heat, strain and reserve the liquid.

Peel and finely chop the other onion and peel and dice the potatoes. Melt the butter in the rinsed out pan and gently sauté the onion for 5 minutes, then add the potatoes and the milk. Simmer gently until the potatoes are soft, then add the reserved fish stock and the mussels, which have been removed from their shells. Blend the flour in a little cold water and stir into the soup. Bring just to the boil and then draw off the heat and add the lemon juice, salt and freshly ground pepper to taste. Ladle into warmed soup bowls and garnish with chopped parsley. Serve with thick slices of wholemeal bread or granary rolls (see pages 109 and 115).

Scallops – or 'clams' as they are usually called on Skye – are gathered at low tide, when found embedded on the top of the sand. They are usually 10-12 cm (4–5 inches) in diameter, and vary in colour from pink to muddy yellow. Nowadays, because of their popularity both at home and on the continental market, the cultivation of the 'Princess' and 'Queen' scallop has been introduced. These are proving to be an interesting new culinary delight in hotels and restaurants throughout the Isle, as well as being of general interest to the visitor.

Here are a few tips on the handling and preparation of scallops (or 'clams') suitable for all recipes listed below:

Wash and scrub the shells, then, holding the scallop (or 'clam') by its hinge, insert a strong knife between the two sides and lever a little apart. Carefully run the knife close to the rounded shell to sever the muscle, and pull the shells apart. Wash thoroughly in cold water, and, with a sharp knife, cut away the black intestine and discard the membrane.

A simple and tasty way to prepare the clam is as follows.

CLAMS BAKED IN BUTTER AND BREADCRUMBS

Detach the corals and white flesh from the shell, and then replace as before. Sprinkle well with wholemeal breadcrumbs, a knob or two of butter, salt, freshly ground pepper and a little chopped parsley. Then put them onto a baking sheet and place in a pre-heated oven 400°F/200°C, for 10-15minutes.

Serve immediately with thin slices of bread and butter.

This is similar to Mussel Chowder, but with a subtle difference in flavour and the addition of a little single cream just before serving.

CLAM CHOWDER *(Serves 6)*

2 onions
1 carrot
Bouquet-garni
Salt and freshly ground pepper
8-10 clams
50 g (2 oz) butter
2 sticks celery
450 g (1 lb) potatoes
Freshly chopped parsley and lovage
150 ml (¼ pint) single cream

Make a *court-bouillon* with 1-1.5 L (2-3 pints) water, one of the onions and the carrot (which have been peeled and sliced) the *bouquet-garni* and a good sprinkling of salt and pepper. Bring to the boil and add the washed and scrubbed clams. Continue boiling until the shells have opened (this takes about 10–15 minutes), then strain and reserve the liquor. Remove the clams from their shells, and roughly chop them.

Melt the butter in a saucepan, then add the *other* onion (peeled and finely chopped) and the diced celery. Sauté together for 5 minutes, then add the peeled and diced potatoes and continue cooking for a further 5 minutes. Add the reserved stock, the parsley and fresh lovage and simmer together until the potato is cooked. Then add the chopped clams, the cream and the freshly chopped parsley and lovage.

Serve with herb and garlic rolls (see page 115).

CLAMS IN A CURRY SAUCE *(Serves 4)*

2 onions
1 carrot
1 bay leaf
1 clove garlic
1 tsp. wine vinegar
8-10 clams
50 g (2 oz) butter
1 tsp. garam masala
½ tsp. cumin seed
1 level tsp. coriander
1 tbsp. flour
1 400 g (14 oz) tin tomatoes (liquidised)
Juice ½ a lemon
1 tbsp. sweet chutney

Make a *court-bouillon* with 600 ml (1 pint) of water, one of the onions and the carrot which have been peeled and sliced, the bay leaf, the finely sliced clove of garlic and the wine vinegar. Bring to the boil and then add in the washed and scrubbed clams. Continue boiling until the shells open (this takes about 10-15 minutes), and then strain and reserve the liquor. Remove the clams from their shells.

Melt the butter in a heavy pan, add the *other* onion which has been peeled and chopped and sauté for a few minutes before adding the garam masala, cumin and coriander. Continue cooking for a further 5 minutes, then add the flour – stirring well – plus 300 ml (½ pint) of the reserved stock. Continue stirring until the mixture thickens, then add the tomatoes, lemon juice and chutney and finally the clams, which have been cut into thick slices leaving the coral whole. Simmer for a further few minutes and serve on a bed of rice which has been cooked, with a bay leaf, in the boiling, salted water.

CLAMS IN CREAM AND SHERRY *(Serves 4)*

This makes a good first course.

6-8 clams
50 g (2 oz) butter
2 tbsp. sherry
2 egg yolks
150 ml (¼ pint) double cream
Salt and freshly ground pepper
Pinch of cayenne pepper
Chopped chives or parsley

Remove the clams from their shells (see directions on page 62) and gently fry them in the butter for 5 minutes. Stir in the sherry and cook for a further 2-3 minutes. Mix the egg yolks with the cream, pour over the clams, season with salt, pepper and cayenne, and leave to heat through until thickened and creamy (but do not boil).

Serve immediately on toast sprinkled with parsley or chives.

CLAMS WITH MUSHROOM AND CHEESE SAUCE *(Serves 4-6)*

8-10 clams
1 large wine glass dry white wine
1 large wine glass water
Sprig of parsley
100 g (4 oz) mushrooms
50 g (2 oz) butter
50 g (2 oz) flour
1 tbsp. lemon juice
50 g (2 oz) Gruyère cheese
4 tbsp. single cream
Salt and freshly ground pepper
225 g (8 oz) mashed potatoes

Wash and scrub the clams and steam in the wine, water, parsley and sliced mushrooms until the shells open (this takes about 10-15 minutes). Strain and reserve the liquor, then remove the clams from their shells and keep in a warm place with the mushrooms.

Melt the butter in a saucepan, stir in the flour and cook for 1 minute. Gradually add the hot stock, stirring well until the sauce thickens and boils, and then add the lemon juice, the grated cheese and salt and pepper to taste. Remove from the heat and add the cream, mushrooms and the clams, which have been sliced leaving the coral whole. Spoon this mixture into the rounded sides of the clam shells (which have been scrubbed clean since cooking). Pipe the mashed potato around the edges, and sprinkle the centre with a little extra cheese. Bake in a pre-heated oven at 375°F/290°C for 15 minutes.

PRINCESS SCALLOPS IN GARLIC BUTTER

Steam the scallops in a *court-bouillon* made with 1.1 L (2 pints) of water, 1 onion and 1 carrot (both peeled and chopped), a *bouquet-garni* and a little salt and pepper. As soon as the shells have opened, remove to a large, warm bowl and serve dipped in garlic butter, which has been made from 50-100 g (2-4 oz) butter, 1-2 cloves garlic (finely chopped), salt and freshly ground black pepper to taste and some chopped parsley.

Hot herb and garlic rolls go well with this (see page 115) or crusty French bread.

PRINCESS SCALLOPS IN WHITE WINE

450 g (1 lb) Princess scallops
25 g (1 oz) butter
1 onion
1 clove garlic
¼ tsp. each sage, thyme and rosemary
1 tbsp. chopped parsley
Juice 1 lime or lemon
½ tsp. sugar
Salt and freshly ground pepper
1 tbsp. cornflour

Steam the scallops in a *court-bouillon* made with 300 ml (½ pint) dry white wine, 300 ml (½ pint) water, 1 onion and 1 carrot (both peeled and sliced), 1 bay leaf and a little salt and pepper. When the shells have opened, strain and reserve the liquor. Remove the scallops from their shells and divide equally between 4 warmed ramekins (or similar small dishes).

Melt the butter in a saucepan and sauté together the finely chopped onion and crushed garlic. Add the herbs, lime or lemon juice, the reserved stock and the sugar. Bring to the boil, season with salt and pepper and thicken with the cornflour which has been mixed with a little cold water to form a thin paste. Continue boiling for another minute, then pour over the scallops, garnish with chopped parsley and serve with hot, crusty bread.

The razor clam, more commonly known as the *razor fish, is* another of the more unusual findings on our shores, and is believed to have taken its name from the old-fashioned, Victorian cut-throat razor which folds into a handle. The pod-like shell is about 8 to 22 cm (3 to 9 inches) long, and sometimes has a brown papery skin concealing a yellowish shell occasionally tinged with a hint of violet.

Like many creatures good for eating they are not easy to catch, and the novice requires a lot of patience and perseverance. Some people prefer to pursue their hunt at night under the light of a full moon, but for the less nocturnal, any time during the day at a low tide can be just as successful, and many times I have seen the experts leaving the shore with several dozen protruding from the top of a large pail.

One clue to knowing where razor fish are most likely to be found is first to look for where shallow depressions can be seen in the sand and then to walk backwards across the shore. This movement, and the pressure exerted by your foot, causes a squirt of water to be sent up by the hidden fish. By inserting a flat, pointed stick into the sand in the opposite direction, you make contact with the shell and thereby stop it, immediately, from withdrawing further. Then, by using your other hand to clear away the sand on top, the fish can be lifted out freely and put in a bucket.

Rather like the winkle, there are not many unusual ways to cook the razor, but here is one method used by the local people:

RAZOR FISH COOKED THE TRADITIONAL WAY

Wash and scrub the razor fish to remove any sand and grit, then place it in a saucepan filled with plenty of boiling, salted water. Bring back to the boil, and continue cooking for about 5 minutes only (cook for too long, and they will become tough and rubbery).

Remove from their shells and eat either with melted butter fried lightly or, for a more special occasion, add to a white sauce. (For myself I would probably use a garlic butter, or combine them in a fish soup in a way similar to the clam chowder. See page 63.)

The last shellfish I make mention of in this chapter is the cockle. As with the others, cockles of the kind are found only at low tide and in groups rather than singly, hence the term 'cockle bed'. They measure anything up to 5 cm (2 inches) long, and are easily distinguished by their fat, ribbed shell which gets bleached white with the sun when empty and left on top of the sand; when alive, they appear dull and often stained.

The best way to gather them is with a garden rake which has flattish prongs, but I suppose they could also be lifted by hand – if you have the patience and are not too ambitious about numbers.

Here are four ways of preparing cockles for the table, one traditional, and the other three with a difference:

COCKLES COOKED THE TRADITIONAL WAY

Leave the cockles to soak overnight in a pail of clean sea water to which a handful of oatmeal has been added (this ensures that all the sand and grit is removed).

Then place them in a saucepan with plenty of boiling, salted water, bring back to the boil, and continue cooking for at least 5 minutes, or until the shells open.

Serve in their shells with vinegar or melted butter.

COCKLE LAYER WITH CHEESE AND POTATO

Cook the cockles as described for the traditional method and remove from their shells.

Butter an ovenproof dish. Put a layer of mashed potato at the bottom, then another of grilled chopped bacon, and another of the cockles. Repeat these layers, finishing up with a layer of grated cheese. Place in a pre-heated oven, 400°F/200°C, for 10 minutes or until the cheese is bubbling hot and turning golden-brown.

Serve with any hot vegetable that is in season.

COCKLE PIE *(Serves 4–6)*

2.3 l (4 pints) cockles
1 onion
2 sticks celery
50 g (2 oz) butter
50 g (2 oz) flour
300 ml (½ pt) milk
Salt & freshly ground pepper
2 tbsp. chopped parsley
225 g (8 oz) homemade flaky pastry, or 1 packet frozen puff pastry

Wash and cook the cockles in the traditional way and remove from their shells reserving the stock. Melt the butter in a saucepan and lightly sauté the peeled and chopped onion and diced celery for about 5 minutes. Slowly add the milk and 300 ml (½ pt) of the reserved stock, stirring all the time until sauce thickens and boils. Season with salt and freshly ground pepper and add the chopped parsley. Lastly add the cockles and pour the mixture into a pie dish. Roll out the pastry and cover the pie dish inserting a pie crock in the middle. Flute the edges, and decorate the centre with pastry leaves. Bake in a pre-heated oven 400°F/200°C for approx 20–25 minutes. Serve with mashed potatoes and vegetables of the season.

COCKLES WITH SPAGHETTI AND TOMATO SAUCE

(Serves 4)

2.3 L (4 pints) cockles
1 onion
1 clove garlic
1 400 g (14 oz) tin tomatoes
1 tsp. fresh basil or ½ tsp. dried
1 tsp. fresh oregano or ½ tsp. dried
1 tsp. sugar
Salt and freshly ground pepper
225 g (8 oz) wholemeal spaghetti

Wash and cook the cockles in the traditional way and remove from their shells.

Sauté the onion and garlic, which have been peeled and finely chopped, in 1 tbsp. oil until soft and transparent, add the tin of tomatoes, the herbs, sugar and salt and pepper and simmer gently together until the sauce thickens. Remove from the heat and add the cockles.

Cook the spaghetti in plenty of boiling, salted water to which a few drops of oil have been added, and then place on a serving dish with the cockle mixture piled on top.

A little grated Parmesan can be added if desired.

SEAWEEDS AND THEIR CULINARY USES

There is a lot of nutritional and mineral goodness to be obtained from the wealth of seaweeds we find on our shores, but alas, too few of us either use them or understand their benefits, and little, if any, appears in our daily diet.

In years gone by, many people from Skye and the other islands, as well as from the west coast of the mainland, used the carragheen for making puddings and the dulse for soups. Their flavoursome qualities, as well as their usefulness as a setting agent (an alternative to gelatine), made them an indispensable item in most crofting households – added to which they contained many valuable medicinal properties, and were effective at soothing digestive problems, relieving sleeplessness and curing minor burns and scalds.

Both carragheen and dulse are best gathered in the early months of summer, and are most commonly found on the rocks at low tide. The carragheen, which has purplish-brown, fan-shaped leaves and flat stems, is easily pulled from its anchorage, as is the dulse which is often found on the same rocks, the reddish-pink fronds making it easily distinguishable from its less colourful neighbours. Ideally, one should use a pair of scissors for cutting, rather than pulling them off the rocks, for if the whole plant is removed it naturally takes a long while for another to grow again.

The method used for drying seaweed involved, firstly, washing it thoroughly in sea water, then spreading it out on a sheet on top of the grass to let the rain wash through and the sun to dry and bleach. Some preferred to hang it up in a fine net bag, and after the weather had bleached it to a whitish-pink, it was then spread on the ground and, when completely dry, was stored in jars for winter use.

Here are two traditional recipes for both dulse and carragheen:

FISH HEAD SOUP WITH DULSE

6 haddock or cod heads
1.1 L (2 pints) water
1 onion
2 carrots
1 small turnip
A good handful of dulse
Salt and pepper

Put the fish heads in a saucepan together with the water and salt, and allow to simmer gently for 1 hour. Strain off the liquor, and discard the heads.

Peel and finely slice the onion, dice the carrots and the turnip, and add these to the reserved liquor. Then, add the dulse and salt and pepper to taste. Bring to the boil, reduce the heat and simmer until the vegetables and dulse are cooked (this takes about 20 minutes).

CARRAGHEEN PUDDING

600 ml (1 pint) milk
50 g (2 oz) sugar
A good handful carragheen
A few drops vanilla essence (optional)

Place the milk in a saucepan, and bring to the boil. Reduce the heat and add the sugar and carragheen. Let it simmer for 10-15 minutes, then add the vanilla and strain through a fine sieve into a wetted mould. Leave in a cool place until set, then turn out on to a plate and serve with cream or the top of the milk.

And now for a few different ideas:

BEANY STEW WITH DULSE AND VEGETABLES

225 g (½ lb) red kidney beans, soya beans and chick peas, mixed
1.1 L (2 pints) water
1 tbsp. oil
2 onions
1 clove garlic
2 carrots, 1 parsnip, 1 small turnip
25 g (1 oz) dulse (soaked in water for 10 minutes)
½ tsp. each dried thyme, sage and basil
2.5 cm (1 inch) root ginger
Salt and freshly ground pepper
1 400 g (14 oz) tin tomatoes
2 tbsp. tomato purée
150 ml (¼ pint) red wine
Juice ½ a lemon
Chopped parsley

Soak the beans overnight. Drain and rinse well. Bring them to the boil in the water, and then simmer for 35-40 minutes or until cooked. Drain and reserve the stock.

Heat the oil in a saucepan, gently fry the peeled and sliced onions and the crushed garlic, and continue cooking for a few minutes. Peel and dice the vegetables and add these to the saucepan together with the dulse, herbs, grated root ginger and salt and pepper. Then, add the tomatoes, tomato purée, red wine and 450 ml (¾ pint) of the stock that the beans were cooked in. Bring to the boil, cover the pan, and simmer for about 30 minutes (if the liquid reduces too quickly, add a little more of the stock). Just before serving, add the lemon juice, and garnish with chopped parsley.

Serve with baked jacket potatoes and a tossed salad.

This is a recipe I use a lot in winter when there is only myself for a meal.

STIR-FRIED VEGETABLES WITH DULSE (*Serves* 4)

15 g (½ oz) dulse (soaked in water for 10 minutes)
1 onion
1 carrot
1 parsnip
½ small turnip
Spinach or any green vegetable that is available
A pinch each of dried thyme, sage and basil
2 tbsp. sunflower oil
1 tbsp. soya sauce
Salt and freshly ground pepper
½ mug bulgar

Heat the oil in a saucepan and add the finely sliced onion, sauté for a few minutes then add the dulse, the peeled and chopped carrot, parsnip and turnip. Sprinkle over the herbs, and salt and pepper to taste, cover tightly with a lid and leave to cook gently for 10–15 minutes. Add the chopped spinach or whatever green vegetable you are using, and the soya sauce, cover and cook for a further 10 minutes. Meanwhile put a little oil in another saucepan, and when hot add the bulgar. Let toast for a few minutes stirring well, then add ½ mug of boiling water and a little salt and leave to cook gently until all the water is absorbed, about 5 minutes. Spoon the cooked bulgar on to a plate and cover with the dulse and vegetable mixture. Garnish with a spoonful of yoghurt and some grated cheese.

STIR-FRIED RICE WITH DULSE AND ALMONDS

(*Serves* 4)

4 tbsp. oil
225 g (8 oz) brown rice
1 bay leaf
1 small onion
25 g (1 oz) dulse (soaked in water for 10 minutes)
1 tbsp. soya sauce
50 g (2 oz) flaked almonds (toasted)

Put 1 tbsp. of oil in a saucepan and, when hot, add the rice. Stir well for a few minutes, then add 300 ml (½ pint) of hot water, the bay leaf and a little salt. Bring to the boil, and then let simmer for 20 minutes or until all the liquid is absorbed and the rice cooked. Remove the bay leaf and allow to cool .

Meanwhile, heat the remaining oil in a heavy frying pan, add the finely sliced onion and sauté for a few minutes. Then, add the dulse, and continue cooking until it softens and darkens in colour. Add the soya sauce and then the rice stirring all together until the mixture is heated through. Lastly, add the toasted almonds and pile on to a warmed serving dish.

This goes well with any egg or fish dish.

Carragheen does not set liquids quite so efficiently as gelatine, but nevertheless can be very acceptable combined with fresh fruits, or made into blancmanges.

FRESH LEMON JELLY WITH GRAPES (*Serves* 4)

2 lemons
75 g (3 oz) sugar
15 g (½ oz) carragheen (soaked in cold water for 30 minutes)
100 g (4 oz) green or black grapes

Finely pare the lemons, taking care not to include any white pith. Put them into a saucepan with the squeezed juice, and add sufficient water to make up to 600 ml (1 pint). Add the sugar, then bring gently to the boil, stirring occasionally, and simmer for 20 minutes. Add the drained carragheen, and continue simmering until the juice thickens, (this takes about 35 to 40 minutes). Place a few grapes in the bottom of 4 small glass dishes and strain over the thickened lemon juice, making sure to press the carragheen down well.

CHOCOLATE BLANCMANGE *(Serves 4)*

600 ml (1 pint) milk
½ tsp. freshly grated nutmeg
100 g (4 oz) dark chocolate
15 g (½ oz) carragheen
(soaked in cold water for 15 minutes)
50 g (2 oz) sugar

Put the milk, nutmeg and chocolate (broken into pieces) into a saucepan, and heat gently until the chocolate has melted. Add the drained carragheen and the sugar, then bring to the boil and simmer for 30 minutes. Strain into a serving dish – pressing the carragheen down firmly – or, for a special occasion, strain first into a jug and then pour into individual glasses or small pots.

Put into the refrigerator to set. Serve with whipped cream and chopped walnuts.

FROM THE HILLS AND HEDGEROWS

Spring, summer and autumn are the months for gathering wild foods, and the island waysides are no exception to all we conjure up of nature's bountiful store.

Whilst the early hours are particularly rewarding – for this is when the dew is still on the grass and the world is silent save for the song of the lark and the cry of the gulls – any time of the day can be pure delight. When the sun is high in the sky, or dipping on the western horizon, there is so much to fill the heart and catch the eye – colours, sounds and smells, all creating an intoxicating mixture of heady impressions guaranteed to lift the heaviest spirit. Like those moments when I am walking on the hills, these are the times when the magic of Skye casts its most bewitching spell.

Apart from collecting the fruits, berries, leaves and mushrooms used for the recipes in this chapter, I can often be found scraping lichen from the rocks, or gathering plants for dyeing the wools used in my weaving; and I welcome the excuse that this gives me to be out in the open air.

With the exception of the section on wild field mushrooms, the following recipes are written in alphabetical order for easy reference.

The wild field mushroom is a rarity here most years, but occasionally, after a mild damp spell in late summer, the easily recognised flat or dome-shaped heads suddenly appear in large numbers in pastures where cattle and sheep have grazed, and the desire to run and pick them is irresistible. Sometimes, on a Sunday afternoon walk along the cliffs to the lighthouse, I have come upon a harvest unawares, and, having neither a basket or bag to put them in, have returned home with pockets brimming, and hands filled. They make a delicious supper simply cooked in butter and served on a thick slice of toast with a rasher or two of bacon, but for some slightly more imaginative ideas for different occasions, here are some suggestions:

MUSHROOM AND LEEK SOUP *(Serves 4)*

225 g (½ lb) mushrooms
1 large leek
25 g (1 oz) butter
25 g (1 oz) wholemeal flour
300 ml (½ pint) milk
450 ml (¾ pint) chicken stock
150 ml (¼ pint) single cream
¼ tsp. ground mace
Salt and freshly ground pepper

Finely slice the mushrooms, and wash and finely slice the leek. Melt the butter in a saucepan and sauté the vegetables for a few minutes. Then add the flour, cook for a further minute before gradually working in the milk and stock and bring to the boil, stirring frequently. Add the mace and salt and pepper to taste, simmer gently until the vegetables are cooked, and then remove the pan from the heat, stir in the cream and pour into warmed bowls. Sprinkle over a little parsley and serve with herb and garlic rolls. (See page 115.)

MUSHROOM PIZZA *(Serves 6)*

For the base:
225 g (8 oz) plain white and wholemeal flours, mixed
1 tsp. salt
150 ml (¼ pint) warm water
1 tsp. sugar
2 tsp. dried yeast
5 tbsp. oil

For the topping
2 tbsp. oil
1 clove garlic
225 g (½ lb) mushrooms
2 tsp. tomato purée
1 tbsp. freshly chopped herbs or ½ tsp. dried herbs
Salt and freshly ground pepper
50 g (2 oz) grated Parmesan cheese or mature cheddar

First make the pizza base. Place the flour and salt in a bowl and put in a warm place whilst preparing the yeast mixture. Pour 150 ml (¼ pint) warm water into a small bowl, add the sugar and sprinkle over the yeast. Put in a warm place to froth (this usually takes about 10 minutes), then add to the flour with the oil and mix together well to form a dough. Turn out on to a floured board, knead well, cover with a cloth and let the dough rise in a warm place for about 1 hour, or until doubled in bulk. Turn again on to a floured board, knead and then flatten with the palm of the hand. Next, pick up the dough and slowly rotate letting it stretch by its own weight but being careful not to allow any holes to appear. When you have a circle about 25cm (10 inches) in diameter place on a greased baking sheet and set aside whilst making the topping.

Heat the oil in a pan and sauté the sliced mushrooms and the peeled and finely chopped garlic for about 2 minutes. Add the tomato purée, herbs and salt and pepper to taste, mix well and spread evenly over the pizza base. Sprinkle with grated cheese and bake in a pre-heated oven 450°F/230°C for 20 minutes or until crusty and golden brown.

MUSHROOM CREAM FLAN

For the pastry:
225 g (8 oz) plain white and wholemeal flours mixed
¼ tsp. salt
50 g (2 oz) margarine
50 g (2 oz) lard
Cold water to mix

For the filling:
25 g (1 oz) butter
225 g (½ lb) mushrooms
2 eggs
150 ml (5 fl oz) natural yoghurt
6 tbsp. single cream
A little grated nutmeg
Salt and freshly ground pepper
2 tsp. either freshly chopped parsley or chives.

To make the pastry, sift the flour and salt into a bowl, rub in the fats with your fingertips until the mixture resembles fine breadcrumbs, add enough water to make a soft dough, then roll it out onto a floured board and place in a 20 cm (8 inch) flan dish.

For the filling, melt the butter in a pan and when hot add the sliced mushrooms and sauté for 5 minutes. Drain well and set the mushrooms aside in a warm place. Whisk the eggs well and add the yoghurt, cream, grated nutmeg and salt and pepper to taste. Scatter the mushrooms onto the base of the flan, pour over the egg mixture, sprinkle with chopped parsley and bake in a pre-heated oven at 375°F/190°C for 30 minutes.

Serve hot or cold with a tossed salad.

MUSHROOM, VEGETABLE AND LENTIL LASAGNE

(Serves 4)

3 tbsp. oil
1 large onion
1 clove garlic
2 carrots
1 parsnip
225 g (8 oz) green or brown lentils
600 ml (1 pint) vegetable stock
1 bay leaf
1 tbsp. chopped, fresh or 1 tsp. dried basil
1 tbsp. chopped, fresh or 1 tsp. dried thyme
Salt and freshly ground pepper
25 g (1 oz) butter
225 g (½ lb) mushrooms
225 g (½ lb) tomatoes
225 g (8 oz) wholemeal or spinach lasagne

For the cheese sauce:
50 g (2 oz) margarine
50 g (2 oz) wholemeal flour
600 ml (1 pint) milk
Salt and freshly ground pepper
½ tsp. ready-made mustard
100 g (4 oz) mature cheddar cheese

For the yoghurt topping:
1 small carton natural yoghurt
1 egg (beaten)
1 tsp. plain white flour
Parmesan cheese

Heat the oil in a heavy pan and sauté the sliced onion and crushed garlic for 5 minutes before adding the peeled and sliced carrots and parsnip. Simmer together for a few more minutes, then add the lentils, stock, bay leaf and herbs and season to taste with salt and pepper. Cover with a lid and continue cooking until the vegetables are soft and the lentils have become a thick purée. In a separate saucepan, melt the butter, and sauté the sliced mushrooms for 5 minutes tossing well. Cut tomatoes into quarters and fold into the lentil mixture together with the mushrooms. Next, make the cheese sauce and cook the lasagne as follows:

Melt the margarine in a saucepan, add the flour and cook together for a few minutes. Gradually add the milk stirring well and as the sauce starts to thicken add the salt, pepper and mustard and bring to the boil. Add the grated cheese and stir until it has dissolved.

Place the lasagne in a large saucepan filled with plenty of boiling salted water to which a little oil has been added. Bring back to the boil and simmer for about 15 minutes or until lasagne is cooked. To assemble the lasagne, select a suitable ovenproof dish, put in first a layer of the mushroom-and-lentil mixture, a layer of cheese sauce, then a layer of the lasagne; and then continue in this order finishing with a layer of the mushroom-and-lentil mixture. Finally, cover with the yoghurt topping, which has been made by blending together the yoghurt, the beaten egg and the flour, mixed to a smooth consistency. Finally, sprinkle with the Parmesan cheese, then bake in a pre-heated oven at 350°F / 180°C for 20 minutes or until golden-brown.

Serve with baked jacket potatoes and a green salad.

MUSHROOMS WITH YOUNG LEEK

Slice the mushrooms, wash and finely slice the leeks, and sauté together in a little hot butter for 5 minutes. Add a small amount of vegetable or chicken stock, and continue cooking until the vegetables are just cooked. Season with salt and freshly ground pepper, soya sauce, and a sprinkling of oregano and thyme, and after letting the flavours blend together for a few minutes, add a little single cream and pile on to a warmed serving dish. Sprinkle with chopped parsley.

The next couple of recipes can only be made when the mushrooms are very plentiful (which did happen one autumn, seven or eight years ago):

MUSHROOM KETCHUP

1.8 kg (4 lbs) mushrooms
75 g (3 oz) sea salt
300 ml (½ pint) red wine vinegar
1 tsp. pickling spices
1 level dsp. chopped onion

Roughly chop the mushrooms, sprinkle with the salt and leave for 24 hours. Strain off the excess liquid (approximately 150 ml (¼ pint)) and replace this with water. Add the vinegar, pickling spices and onion, and simmer in a preserving pan for 2 ½ hours. Liquidise, pour into warm bottles and seal well.

This ketchup will keep for several years.

MUSHROOM CHUTNEY

1.4 kg (3 lbs) mushrooms
450 g (1 lb) cooking apples
225 g (½ lb) onions
15 g (½ oz) root ginger
225 g (8 oz) sultanas
225 g (8 oz) demerara sugar
1 tsp. salt
450 ml (¾ pint) red or white wine vinegar
½ tsp. cayenne pepper
1 tsp. mustard powder

Roughly chop the mushrooms, peel and quarter the apples, and skin and roughly slice the onions. Mince these ingredients together and place in a preserving pan with the ginger, bruised and tied in a muslin, and all the remaining ingredients. Bring to the boil and simmer for about 1 ½ hours until the liquid has evaporated. Then remove the muslin bag, cool for a minute, and then pour into warmed pots and seal in the normal way.

Up in the high hills amongst the heather, one can occasionally find a small, purplish berry known to the local people as the blaeberry. In years gone by they were normally gathered before the sheep were dipped in the month of August, thus avoiding any harmful chemicals penetrating the fruit and spoiling the flavour. Nowadays with different agricultural methods, it matters less and berries can be gathered well into September, or for as long as they remain firm and ripe.

The fruit has a rich red juice, and like the blackcurrant, contains a high percentage of vitamin C. They can be eaten raw whilst gathering, or put in a bowl with sugar and cream, but watch for the purplish dye that quickly stains both hands and teeth. More popular is to cook the berries and then make them into pies, crumbles, jams and jellies. They also mix well with apples, so if you only find a small number don't despair.

Here is an American recipe, brought home from my travels there several years ago. I have substituted blaeberries for blueberries.

BLAEBERRY MUFFINS

100 g (4 oz) butter
100 g (4 oz) sugar
2 eggs
225 g (8 oz) plain flour
1 tsp. baking powder
Pinch of salt
175 g (6 oz) blaeberries

Cream together the butter and the sugar until light and fluffy. Add the beaten eggs a little at a time, alternating with a spoonful of the sifted flour, baking powder and salt. When all the flour has been incorporated, add the blaeberries and spoon the whole lot into well-greased muffin tins. Bake in a preheated oven 400°F/200°C for 20 minutes.

BRAMBLE AND CINNAMON MOUSSE *(Serves 4)*

450 g (1 lb) brambles
Juice 1 lemon
1 stick cinnamon
100 g (4 oz) caster sugar
3 tbsp. water
15 g (½ oz) gelatine
150 ml (¼ pint) double cream
2 egg whites

Wash the brambles, and put them into a saucepan with the lemon juice, cinnamon stick and the sugar. Place them over a low heat, simmer gently for about 10 minutes – or until the brambles are soft – then remove the cinnamon stick and place on one side.

Put the water in a small bowl, sprinkle over the gelatin, leave for 5 minutes and then add to the hot fruit, stirring until it has dissolved. Liquidise, and then sift the fruit into a large bowl, leaving it to get cold.

Lightly whisk the cream, then the egg whites (until stiff), and fold first the cream and then the egg whites into the purée, making sure that they are well blended. Pour into a serving dish and place in the refrigerator until set.

Decorate with whipped cream and a few extra brambles.

BRAMBLE AND APPLE SPONGE PUDDING *(Serves 4)*

450 g (1 lb) brambles
225 g (½ lb) cooking apples
150 g (5 oz) caster sugar
100 g (4 oz) butter
2 eggs
100 g (4 oz) self-raising flour (sifted)
Grated rind 1 lemon

Wash the brambles, peel, core and slice the apples, then place together at the bottom of a buttered, ovenproof dish and sprinkle over 25 g (1 oz) of the sugar.

Cream the butter with the remaining 100 g (4 oz) of sugar until light and fluffy, and beat in the eggs one at a time, adding a few spoonfuls of flour to prevent the mixture from curdling. Then, add the lemon rind and the remaining flour, mixing to a soft consistency. Spread this over the prepared fruit and place in a pre-heated oven, 375°F / 190°C, for 30-35 minutes.

Serve with whipped cream.

BRAMBLE AND LEMON ICE CREAM *(Serves 4)*

450 g (1 lb) brambles
1 lemon
3 small eggs
75 g (3 oz) caster sugar
150 ml (¼ pint) double cream

Wash the brambles, place them in a saucepan with the grated lemon rind and juice and simmer gently for about 10 minutes. When the fruit is soft, remove from the heat, liquidise and then pass through a sieve to remove the pips.

Separate the eggs, whisk the yolks together with the sugar until thick and pale in colour, then fold in the fruit purée. Lightly whip the cream and then whisk the egg whites until stiff. Fold first the cream and then the egg whites into the fruit mixture and pour into a polythene container.

Freeze for at least 6 hours, and serve garnished with a few fresh brambles and a finger of shortbread. (See page 135.)

BRAMBLE JELLY CONSERVE

1.8 kg (4 lbs) brambles
600 ml (1 pint) water
Juice 2 lemons
Sugar

Wash the brambles and place in a preserving pan with the juice of the lemons and the water. Bring to the boil and simmer gently until the fruit is soft. Remove from the heat and strain through a jelly bag. Allow 450 g (1 lb) sugar for each 600 ml (1 pint) of juice, and return them to the rinsed pan. Bring to the boil, and boil rapidly for about 10 minutes or until the setting point is reached. To test, put a little on a saucer and, when cold, tip to one side; if a slight skin forms the jelly is cooked.

Pour into warmed jars and seal in the normal way.

BRAMBLE AND APPLE JAM

1 kg (2 lbs) brambles
675 g (1 ½ lbs) cooking apples
1.4 kg (3 lbs) granulated sugar
300 ml (½ pint) water

Wash the brambles and peel, core and slice the apples. Place in a preserving pan together with the water, and bring to the boil. Simmer gently until the fruit is soft, then stir in the sugar, and continue stirring until the sugar is dissolved. Bring back to the boil and boil rapidly for about 15 minutes. Draw pan off the heat and test for setting.

Pour into warmed jars and seal in the normal way.

DANDELION, CELERY AND POTATO SALAD *(Serves 6)*

450 g (1 lb) new potatoes
4 sticks celery
25 g (1 oz) dandelion leaves

For the mayonnaise:
1 egg yolk
¼ tsp. ready-made mustard
freshly ground pepper
150 ml (¼ pint) sunflower and olive oil, mixed
1 dsp. white wine vinegar

Boil the potatoes in their skins and, when cooked, allow to get cold. Remove the skins, roughly dice and place in a bowl together with the celery (diced) and the dandelion leaves (finely chopped).

Make the mayonnaise by putting the egg yolk into a blender with the mustard and a good grinding of pepper. Mix together briefly, then add the oil, drop by drop, and the vinegar. If the consistency looks too thick, add a little boiling water.

Pour the mayonnaise over the potatoes, celery and dandelion leaves, mix well, and pile onto a serving dish and sprinkle with fresh parsley.

DANDELION, CASHEW NUT AND MUSHROOM SALAD *(Serves 4)*

25 g (1 oz) dandelion leaves
100 g (4 oz) mushrooms
50 g (2 oz) mung-bean sprouts
225 g (½ lb) tomatoes
100 g (4 oz) cashew nuts

For the dressing:
4 tbsp. sunflower and olive oil, mixed
2 tbsp. white wine vinegar
¼ tsp. mustard powder
1 clove garlic (crushed)
Salt and freshly ground pepper

Finely chop the dandelion leaves, and thinly slice the mushrooms. Place in a bowl with the mung-bean sprouts, the tomatoes (which have been cut into quarters) and the cashew nuts.

Put the rest of the ingredients into a screw-top jar, shake well and pour over the salad. Toss this well and serve with a few toasted pumpkin seeds sprinkled over the top – or, if these are not available, a little chopped parsley.

DANDELION COFFEE

This may be viewed with suspicion by many, but, unlike caffeine, it does not cause wakefulness or heartburn. It is good for digestion and rheumatism, and is a pleasant alternative to ordinary coffee.

Collect a small pailful of freshly dug dandelion roots. Wash them well, then roughly chop, put on a tray, and place in the airing cupboard, or another suitably warm place, until thoroughly dried out. Grind in a coffee grinder, spread out on a baking tray and place in a pre-heated oven, 350°F/180°C, to roast for 6-8 minutes. Store in a screw-top jar.

To make the coffee, place 25 g (1 oz) of the roasted grounds in 600 ml (1 pint) of boiling water, leave to infuse for 5-10 minutes and then strain into a warmed coffee jug.

Serve black or with milk and sugar, according to taste.

ELDERFLOWER FRITTERS WITH WILD RASPBERRY SAUCE *(Serves 4)*

75 g (3 oz) plain flour
pinch salt
2 eggs
1 tbsp. olive oil
6 tbsp. elderflower wine (see page 142)
8 sprigs elderflowers

For the sauce:
350 g (¾ lb) wild raspberries
1 tbsp. caster sugar

Put the sifted flour and salt into a bowl. Make a well in the centre and beat in the eggs one at a time. Beat in the oil and then the elderflower wine and continue beating until smooth. Leave to stand for 30 minutes.

Meanwhile make the sauce, by placing the raspberries together with the sugar in a saucepan. Heat gently until the juices begin to run, and when the sugar has dissolved and the berries are slightly soft, liquidise in a blender and then sift to remove the pips.

To make the fritters. Heat a pan of oil (olive or sunflower) and, when hot, take a sprig of the elderflowers and dip the whole head into the batter. Then, fry in the oil until crisp and golden-brown. Drain on absorbent paper and serve hot, with the raspberry sauce served in a separate bowl.

ELDERFLOWER SORBET *(Serves 4)*

300 ml (½ pint) water
1 level tsp. gelatine
A good handful elderflowers
1 lemon
150 g (5 oz) caster sugar
1 egg white

Put 1 tbsp. of the water in a small bowl and sprinkle over the gelatine. Put the remaining water, the elderflowers, thinly pared lemon rind and the sugar into a saucepan, and stir over a gentle heat until the sugar has dissolved. Bring to the boil and then lower the heat and simmer for 5 minutes. Remove from the heat, add the soaked gelatine and stir until dissolved. Stir in the lemon juice and allow to cool completely. Strain to remove the elderflowers and lemon rind and pour into a polythene container.

Freeze until icy at the edges, and turn out into a bowl; whisk the egg white until stiff, then whisk the two together until thick and snowy. Return to the polythene container and freeze for several hours until quite firm.

Scoop into small glass dishes and serve immediately.

ELDERFLOWER CORDIAL

1 lemon
50 g (2 oz) sugar
2 heads of elderflowers in full bloom

Finely pare the lemon making sure not to include any white pith. Place in a heatproof jug, add the lemon juice, sugar and elderflowers and then pour over 900 ml (1 ½ pints) boiling water. Stir well and leave to get completely cold. Strain into another jug and keep in the refrigerator.

ELDERBERRY AND APPLE TART *(Serves 6)*

100 g (4 oz) butter
50 g (2 oz) caster sugar
1 egg yolk
75 g (3 oz) plain white flour
75 g (3 oz) wholemeal plain flour
¼ tsp. salt
1 tbsp. water
Beaten egg or milk for glazing

For the filling:
450 g (1 lb) cooking apples
4 sprays ripe elderberries (removed from their stalks)
2 tbsp. light brown sugar
½ tsp. cinnamon

Beat the butter and sugar until light and fluffy, add the egg yolk, the sifted flour, salt and water. Knead together until a dough is formed, and place in the refrigerator for several hours.

Divide in half and roll one half out thinly to cover a 20 cm (8 inch) pie dish. Arrange the peeled, cored and sliced apples over the base, cover with the elderberries and sprinkle over the sugar and cinnamon. Cover with the remaining half of the pastry, flute the edges and make a small hole in the centre to let the steam escape. Brush with the beaten egg or milk, sprinkle with demerara sugar and bake in a pre-heated oven at 400°F / 200°C for 20 minutes.

Serve with whipped cream.

(A shortcrust pastry could be substituted for the above method if preferred.)

ELDERBERRY WINE JELLY *(Serves 4)*

300 ml (½ pint) water
15 g (½ oz) gelatine
100 g (4 oz) caster sugar
Thinly pared rind 1 orange
Thinly pared rind ½ a lemon
300 ml (½ pint) elderberry wine (see page 142)

Put 2 tbsp. of the water into a small bowl, sprinkle over the gelatine and leave for 5 minutes. Pour the remaining water into a saucepan and add the sugar and the thinly pared orange and lemon rinds. Stir over a low heat until the sugar is dissolved, then simmer for 10 minutes. Remove from the heat, add the soaked gelatine and stir until dissolved. Stir in the elderberry wine, and strain into a wetted mould. Leave to set in a cool place and just before serving, put it into a bowl of hot water for a few seconds and turn it out on to a serving dish.

Serve with a jug of single cream.

ELDERBERRY AND APPLE JELLY CONSERVE

1 kg (2 lbs) cooking apples
1.8 kg (4 lbs) elderberries
1.1 L (2 pints) water
Sugar

Wash the apples and cut them up without peeling. Put the apples and elderberries in a preserving pan, add the water and simmer until soft. Strain through a jelly bag and leave to drip.

Measure the liquid and use 450 g (1 lb) sugar for every 600 ml (1 pint) of juice. Return to the rinsed out pan, allow the sugar to dissolve over a low heat, then bring to the boil and boil rapidly until setting point is reached. Pour into warmed jars and seal in the usual way.

ELDERBERRY PUNCH

This is very good on a cold winter's evening when returning from a hill-walk or a day at the winkles!

1 bottle elderberry wine (see page 142)
1 cinnamon stick
2.5 cm (1 inch) piece root ginger
a little freshly grated nutmeg
½ tsp. allspice
4 cloves
150 ml (¼ pint) brandy (optional)

Bruise the ginger and tie it in a muslin, then put all the ingredients except the brandy in a saucepan, bring gently to the boil and simmer for 15 minutes. Add the brandy (if used), and strain into warmed earthenware mugs or glasses.

When I first came to my present home the garden was covered with ground elder – or 'bishop's weed', to give it the local name – and I was never more surprised and delighted to discover that it was edible. Before the days when I could grow my own green vegetables, this prolific weed provided a welcome change from the often travel-weary cabbages available in the shops during those days. It is rich in iron, and often recommended for rheumatic pains and sciatica. The leaves and stems are best picked in the spring or early summer when still bright green and tender. If boiled as a vegetable it is much like spinach, but here are two more exciting variations:

POTATO AND GROUND ELDER SOUP *(Serves 4)*

1 onion
25 g (1 oz) butter
450 g (1 lb) potatoes
½ small swede or turnip
2 carrots
1.1 L (2 pints) chicken stock
1 bay leaf
1 dsp. of freshly picked mixed herbs or 1 tsp. dried herbs of your choice
Salt and freshly ground pepper
A good handful of freshly picked ground elder

Peel and slice the onion, sauté in the butter in a large saucepan until transparent, then add the peeled and diced potatoes and continue cooking for 5 minutes. Next, add the peeled and diced swede and carrots, the chicken stock, bay leaf, mixed herbs and salt and pepper to taste. Bring to the boil, put in the ground elder leaves and simmer for about 15-20 minutes or until all the vegetables are cooked. Liquidise, and serve with croûtons and a sprinkling of fresh parsley.

GROUND ELDER AND CHICKPEA SALAD *(Serves 4)*

225 g (8 oz) chickpeas
A good handful ground elder leaves
150 ml (¼ pint) natural yoghurt
½ tsp. ground coriander
½ tsp. ground cumin
1 tsp. freshly chopped sage or ½ tsp. dried sage
1 clove garlic
Juice ½ a lemon
Freshly ground pepper

Soak the beans overnight, strain and simmer gently in a saucepan of fresh water for about 1 hour or until cooked.

Drain and allow to cool. Finely chop the ground elder leaves, mix the yoghurt with the spices, garlic, lemon juice and pepper, and combine all ingredients.

Pile into a serving dish and sprinkle with fresh parsley.

The hawthorn is another of our wayside findings unlikely to have an edible quality, especially with its prickly stem. However, when the leaves, blossoms and berries are gathered at the right time of year, it is surprising what can be done with them. Here are a few suggestions:

HAWTHORN LEAF AND BACON DUMPLING *(Serves 4)*

75 g (3 oz) shredded suet
225 g (8 oz) self-raising wholemeal flour
25 g (1 oz) young hawthorn leaves gathered in spring
100 g (4 oz) chopped bacon
100 g (4 oz) chopped lamb's liver
2 onions
Salt and freshly ground pepper

Mix the suet with the flour and add enough water to make a firm dough. Roll out into an oblong and spread on the finely chopped hawthorn leaves , the bacon, liver and sliced onions. Sprinkle with salt and freshly ground pepper, and roll it up, sealing the edges well. Dip a pudding cloth in boiling water, flour it thoroughly and wrap it round the roll. Tie the ends securely and steam for 2 ½ hours.

Serve with tomato sauce. (See page 24.)

This slightly bitter-sweet jelly is good with lamb or venison, but is also rather nice with scones and crowdie. The elderberries can be gathered when in season and put in the freezer.

HAWTHORN AND ELDERBERRY JELLY

1 kg (2 lbs) hawthorn berries gathered after the first frost
450 g (1 lb) elderberries
750 g (1 ½ lbs) cooking apples
1.7 L (3 pints) water
Sugar

Wash the hawthorn berries and the elderberries, and remove any stalks. Chop the apples without peeling and coring and put all together in a preserving pan with the water. Bring gently to the boil and simmer for about 1 hour or until thick and pulpy. Place in a jelly bag and leave to drip for several hours or overnight.

Measure the liquid and use 450 g (1 lb) sugar for every 600 ml (1 pint) of juice. Return to the rinsed preserving pan, allow the sugar to dissolve over a low heat, then bring to the boil and boil rapidly until the setting point is reached.

Pour into warmed jars and seal them in the normal way.

HAWTHORN FLOWER WINE CUP

1 bottle hawthorn flower wine (see page 141)
A few lemon balm leaves
Thinly pared rind 1 orange

Put all the ingredients into a jug, cover and leave in a cool place for 24 hours. Strain and chill lightly before serving.

The hazel tree grows prolifically in the more sheltered and wooded areas of Skye, but can also occasionally be found in quite exposed areas like cliff faces and open moorland.

We gather the nuts in late summer and autumn, and after having been dried thoroughly in a warm atmosphere, they can be stored in sealed tins for up to 6 months.

HAZELNUT CROWDIE AND FRESH PEACH SALAD

(Serves 4)

4 fresh peaches
4 sticks celery
450 g (1 lb) crowdie
4 tbsp. single cream
A pinch cayenne pepper
A few drops Tabasco sauce
Salt and freshly ground pepper
100 g (4 oz) shelled hazelnuts (toasted)
1 small crispy lettuce

Plunge the peaches into boiling water for a few minutes, and then peel off their skins, cut into quarters and set aside.

Dice the celery. Mix the crowdie with the cream, cayenne pepper and Tabasco sauce, season with salt and pepper and add the hazelnuts, peaches and the celery. Mix together well and pile on to a finely shredded bed of lettuce. Sprinkle with fresh parsley.

This delicious recipe for honey and hazelnut cake was given to me when I worked in a restaurant on Skye several years ago. Too extravagant for every day use but perfect for a special occasion.

HONEY AND HAZELNUT CAKE

225 g (½ lb) honey
6 eggs
100 g (4 oz) plain flour (sifted)
100 g (4 oz) hazelnuts
A little single cream for mixing

Grease and line a 20 cm (8 inch) round cake tin. Put the honey into a jar and stand in a saucepan of hot water until it softens to a pouring consistency.

Separate the eggs and put the yolks into a large bowl and beat well. Then pour over the warmed honey and gradually add the sifted flour, the hazelnuts (which have been pounded in a mortar with a little caster sugar) and enough cream to bind the mixture together. Whisk the egg whites until very stiff and fold these in carefully. When smooth and thoroughly blended, pour into the prepared cake tin and bake in a pre-heated oven at 350°F / 180°C for 40-45 minutes. When cold, turn the cake out, slice in half and fill with freshly whipped cream, flavoured with a little strong coffee and a measure of Drambuie.

Refrigerate until ready to use.

HAZELNUT AND APRICOT MERINGUE CAKE *(Serves 6)*

100 g (4 oz) shelled hazelnuts
4 egg whites
200 g (8 oz) caster sugar
½ tsp. vinegar
1 tsp. cornflour

For the filling:
100 g (4 oz) dried apricots
1 tsp. brown sugar
1 orange
½ inch stick cinnamon
2 tsp. arrowroot
2 tbsp. brandy (optional)
300 ml (½ pint) double cream

Lightly oil and line 2 × 7 inch (17cm) cake tins. Soak the apricots.

Put hazelnuts on a baking sheet and place in a pre-heated oven 375°F/190°C for 5-10 minutes. Remove the papery brown skins by rubbing them in a teacloth and grind finely in a coffee grinder. Whisk the egg whites until stiff, then add half the sugar one tablespoon at a time, whisking well between each addition. Mix the remaining sugar with the ground hazelnuts and fold this lightly into the meringue with the vinegar and cornflour. Divide the mixture between the two tins and place on the middle shelf of the oven and cook for approximately 30 minutes.

Meanwhile make the filling: drain the apricots, snip into smallish pieces and place in a saucepan together with the grated rind and juice of the orange, the cinnamon stick and the brown sugar. Simmer gently until soft then thicken with the arrowroot blended with a little cold water. Stir in the brandy and leave to get cold.

When the meringue is cooked, allow to cool in the tin, then loosen the sides and turn out onto a wire rack. When completely cold, cover one half with the apricot mixture, and the other half with the whipped cream. Sandwich the two together, dust with icing sugar and refrigerate for several hours before serving.

For a variation, put half the whipped cream only in the centre of the cake and the other half on top and sprinkle with a few chopped nuts.

CRUNCHY HAZELNUT AND BLACKCURRANT SLICES

225 g (8 oz) ground hazelnuts
225 g (8 oz) butter
100 g (4 oz) wholemeal plain flour
100 g (4 oz) plain white flour
225 g (8 oz) demerara sugar
Blackcurrant and applemint jam (see page 46)

Put all the ingredients into a bowl, except for the blackcurrant jam, and mix them together well so that they resemble breadcrumbs.

Pour half the mixture into a lightly oiled Swiss-roll tin and press down firmly and evenly. Spread a thin layer of the jam on top, and then sprinkle over the other half of the crumb mixture, pressing down firmly with a damp fork.

Bake in a pre-heated oven, 350°F/180°C, for about 30 minutes or until golden-brown. Remove from the oven and cool for a few minutes before marking into squares. When completely cold, carefully lift from the tin and store in an airtight container.

In mid summer, the meadowsweet grows in the fields round about my house, so is easily gathered for culinary purposes as well as for dyeing the wool I use for weaving. It has a sweet, almost honey-like flavour, so is useful for sweetening tart fruits; and it makes a refreshing fragrant tea.

MEADOWSWEET WITH WORCESTERBERRIES *(Serves 4)*

450 g (1 lb) worcesterberries
110 ml (4 fl oz) worcesterberry wine (see page 145)
1 tbsp. honey
4 heads meadowsweet flowers

Top and tail the worcesterberries. Put the wine and honey into a saucepan, heat gently, add the worcesterberries and the meadowsweet flowers then cover and simmer for 15 minutes until soft but still whole. Discard the meadowsweet flowers and serve with custard or whipped cream.

MEADOWSWEET WINE SYLLABUB *(Serves 6)*

110 ml (4 fl oz) meadowsweet wine (see page 144)
1 lemon
1 tbsp. clear honey
300 ml (½ pint) double cream

Put the wine and the thinly pared lemon rind into a bowl and leave to stand overnight so that the wine takes up the flavour of the lemon.

Remove the rind and add the lemon juice, the slightly warmed honey and the cream. Whisk until thick and light, and spoon into individual glasses. Place in the refrigerator for several hours and serve with sponge fingers.

MEADOWSWEET TEA

Infuse 1 fresh flowerhead, or 1 tsp. dried flowers and leaves (mixed together), in 300 ml (½ pint) of boiling water, and then add a slice of lemon and 1 tsp. honey.

Another prolific weed that I discovered when I came to live here was the nettle. My despair was lessened a little, however, when I discovered that it can be used in a delicious soup. This recipe comes from a near neighbour, Eva Lambert, who mentions it in her book *The Garden Grows*.

NETTLE SOUP *(Serves 4)*

450 g (1 lb) young nettles (chopped)
25 g (1 oz) butter, or enough
oil to cover the bottom of the pan
1 large onion (sliced)
2 large potatoes (peeled and cubed)
Salt and freshly ground pepper
1.1 L (2 pints) whey; or,
600 ml (1 pint) milk (sour if possible)
and 600 ml (1 pint) water; or, stock
1 clove garlic (crushed)

Heat the oil (or melt the butter) in a large saucepan. Cook the onion until transparent, then add the washed and chopped nettles, the potatoes and the salt and pepper. Cover tightly and cook for about 15-20 minutes or until the potato is soft. (If the vegetables start to stick, add enough water to keep them from burning.) When all is cooked, add the whey (or the milk and water or the stock) and the crushed garlic. Heat to simmering point and serve with a sprinkling of grated cheese and thick slices of toast. Sometimes I prefer to liquidise it for a smoother consistency.

NETTLE AND POTATO CAKES

50 g (1 lb) potatoes
1 onion
25 g (1 oz) butter
1 egg yolk
Salt and freshly ground pepper
225 g (8 oz) nettle tops

Boil the potatoes in their skins with the peeled onion until they are soft. Drain, cool slightly and then remove the skins from the potatoes. Return them to the pan and mash together with the onion, butter, egg yolk and salt and pepper (to taste).

Meanwhile, put the washed and chopped nettles into a saucepan containing a little boiling, salted water and cook until soft. Drain well, squeezing out any excess water and add the nettles to the potato mixture. Blend them together well, shape into rounds on a floured board and fry in dripping or sunflower oil until golden-brown on each side.

Serve with cold meat, bacon or a fried egg.

NETTLE BEER

1 kg (2 lbs) young nettles
15 g (½ oz) root ginger
4.5 L (1 gallon) water
2 lemons
450 g (1 lb) demerara sugar
25 g (1 oz) cream of tartar
1 tbsp. dried yeast

Wash the nettles, chop roughly and place in a large pan, with the bruised ginger (tied in a muslin) and the water. Bring to the boil and simmer for 20 minutes. Strain into a bucket containing the lemon peel (which has been finely pared, leaving out any white pith), the juice, sugar and cream of tartar. Stir well and when cool add the yeast.

Keep covered with a thick cloth or lid in a warm place for 3 days. Rack, bottle, cork and keep for 1 week before drinking.

Peppermint and water mint are the most common of the wild mints found in the burns and wet meadow areas around North Skye. I introduced the peppermint into my garden in the early days before establishing the more usual garden varieties, and found it a most useful accompaniment to salads, popping into a pot whilst cooking new potatoes or fresh peas, or for using either to brew a refreshing beverage or to make this delicious summer dessert:

PEPPERMINT AND LEMON WATER ICE *(Serves 6)*

300 ml (½ pint) water
2 handfuls peppermint, stripped from its stalks
2 lemons
100 g (4 oz) granulated sugar

Put the water, peppermint leaves, finely pared lemon rinds and sugar into a saucepan and heat gently until the sugar has dissolved. Then, boil rapidly for about 5 minutes, remove from the heat and cool completely. Remove the peppermint leaves and the lemon rind then pour into a polythene container and place in the freezer.

After about an hour, remove from the freezer and beat well. Repeat this twice more, and then put into the refrigerator for 30 minutes before serving.

PEPPERMINT TEA

Place 2 tbsp. freshly chopped peppermint or 1 tbsp dried in 225 ml (8 fl oz) boiling water and leave to infuse for 10 minutes in a warm place. Sweeten with honey to taste.

The following two recipes are a pleasant accompaniment to roast lamb.

WATER MINT JELLY

1.4 kg (3 lbs) cooking apples
450 ml (¾ pint) water
150 ml (¼ pint) red wine vinegar
Light brown sugar
6 tbsp. water mint

Coarsely chop the apples and place in a preserving pan with the water and vinegar. Bring to the boil, and simmer gently for 45 minutes until soft, mashing down occasionally. Strain through a jelly bag and leave to drip for several hours or overnight.

Measure the liquid and add 225 g (8 oz) of sugar for every 300 ml (½ pint). Put the liquid into the rinsed pan, bring to the boil and add the sugar, stirring until it dissolves. Return to the boil and boil rapidly until the setting point is reached. Take the pan from the heat and stir in the finely chopped mint . Cool the jelly and stir it from time to time to distribute the mint evenly. Pour into warmed pots and cover in the usual way.

WATER MINT SAUCE WITH LEMON

2 tbsp. fresh water mint
1 dsp. light brown sugar
Juice of ½ lemon

Finely chop the mint and mix together with the sugar. Pour over sufficient boiling water to be soaked up by the mint then add the lemon juice and leave for a while to infuse. Taste for flavour and add more lemon juice or sugar as required.

Regrettably, I have not yet been able to establish enough shelter in my garden to grow raspberries successfully, but during the summer months it is not unusual to see wild ones growing in the hedgerows, and these have a particularly lovely flavour. Here is one of my favourite ways of preparing them:

WILD RASPBERRIES WITH YOGHURT TOPPING

Wild raspberries
Equal amounts of natural yoghurt and double cream
Light brown muscavado sugar

In a glass dish, place a generous layer of raspberries. Whip the cream and yoghurt together and place over the raspberries. Sprinkle liberally with soft brown sugar making sure the surface is completely covered. Place in the refrigerator and leave for 8 hours – or overnight is even better. The sugar will melt and form a crunchy top.

WILD RASPBERRY FLAN *(Serves 4–6)*

100 g (4 oz) plain flour
Pinch of salt
25 g (1 oz) butter
25 g (1 oz) white cooking fat
15 g (½ oz) caster sugar
1½ tbsp. milk

For the filling:
8 oz wild raspberries
2 tsp. arrowroot

Sift the flour and salt into a bowl, add the butter and white cooking fat and lightly rub together until mixture resembles fine breadcrumbs. Add in the sugar and sufficient milk for the dough to knit together. Roll out on a floured board and line an 8 inch (20cm) flan tin. Bake blind in a pre-heated oven 400°F/200°C for 15 minutes remembering to remove the covering for the last 5 minutes.

When the flan case is cold carefully remove from the tin and place on a serving dish. Fill the centre with the raspberries and cover with the arrowroot glaze which has been made by combining the arrowroot with a little cold water, adding it to a pan containing 150 ml (¼ pint) water and stirring continuously until mixture thickens and clears. A few toasted almonds sprinkled over the top give an attractive and crunchy finish.

WILD RASPBERRY MACAROON MERINGUE *(Serves 4)*

225 g (8 oz) freshly picked wild raspberries
225 g (8 oz) crushed macaroons
3 egg whites
2 tbsp. caster sugar

Crush the raspberries and add the macaroons. Whisk the egg whites until stiff and add the sugar one spoonful at a time, whisking well between each addition. Then fold in the raspberry-and-macaroon mixture and turn into a greased ovenproof dish. Bake in a pre-heated oven at 350°F/180°C for 20 minutes.

Serve with whipped cream.

WILD RASPBERRY MERINGUE PUDDING *(Serves 4)*

450 g (1 lb) freshly picked wild raspberries
3-4 individual sponge cakes (home made if possible)
2 large eggs
100 g (4 oz) caster sugar
300 ml (½ pint) milk
1 tsp. vanilla essence

Place the raspberries in the bottom of a buttered, ovenproof dish. Cut the sponge cakes lengthways and place over the top.

Separate the eggs. Place the yolks in a bowl with 50 g (2 oz) of the sugar and beat well. Heat the milk slightly in a saucepan and pour on to the eggs and sugar, stirring well. Return the mixture to the rinsed-out saucepan and continue stirring over a low heat until the custard thickens but does not boil. Add the vanilla essence, then pour over the raspberries and the sponge cake.

Whisk the egg whites until stiff, gradually adding the remaining 50 g (2 oz) sugar. Pile on top of the pudding and bake in a pre-heated oven at 300°F/160°C for 30 minutes.

Serve hot with or without cream.

WILD RASPBERRY CONSERVE

1 kg (2 lbs) freshly picked raspberries
1 small handful raspberry leaves
1 kg (2 lbs) granulated sugar

Place the raspberries and raspberry leaves in a preserving pan and place over a gentle heat until the juices begin to run and the fruit begins to break up. Add the warmed sugar and stir until dissolved. Bring to the boil and boil rapidly for 5 minutes. Draw the pan from the heat, remove the leaves and test for setting. Pour into small, warmed jars and seal them in the usual way.

ROSE PETAL AND APPLE JELLY

1 kg (2 lbs) cooking apples
600 ml (1 pint) water
Thinly pared rind and juice ½ a lemon
Granulated sugar
25-50 g (1-2 oz) fresh rose petals

Peel, core and slice the apples and put them into a saucepan with the water and lemon rind. Bring to the boil and simmer for 1 ½ hours. Strain the contents through a jelly bag and leave hanging up for several hours or overnight.

Measure the liquid and add 225 g (8 oz) of sugar for every 300 ml (½ pint) of juice. Put into a clean pan, add the rose petals and the lemon juice, and stir over a gentle heat until the sugar has dissolved. Bring to the boil and boil rapidly for about 10 minutes. Test for setting, and strain into small, warmed jars. Seal them in the usual way.

This syrup is very rich in vitamin C, and a teaspoon taken every day during winter helps to keep colds away. It can also be used to pour over puddings.

ROSEHIP SYRUP

450 g (1 lb) rosehips
1.7 L (3 pints) boiling water
275 g (10 oz) sugar for each 600 ml (1 pint) juice

Chop or mince the rosehips and put them immediately into a pan containing the boiling water. Simmer for about 5 minutes then leave to stand for 15 minutes.

Strain and measure the liquid and add the sugar. Return to the heat. When the sugar has dissolved, pour into pre-heated bottling jars – leaving a space of about 2.5 cm (1 inch) at the top of each bottle – and seal. Allow to cool, and then stand the jars on a wooden rack inside a large pan, slacken the screw bands slightly and very slowly bring to simmering point; continue simmering for 20-30 minutes, depending on the bottle size. Remove carefully, put them onto a wooden surface and tighten the screw bands. This method helps to retain the vitamin C.

ROSEHIP TEA

Place the rosehips on a baking tray and put them in the airing cupboard or a similarly warm, dry place until they are thoroughly dried out. Then, crush with a rolling pin, or a pestle and mortar, and store in an airtight jar.

To make the tea, place 1 heaped tsp. in a cup, pour over the boiling water, leave to infuse for a few minutes and sweeten with honey to taste.

It is better to pick the berries for this jelly when they are just beginning to turn from orange to bright red; left too long, they become bitter and the set is not so good.

ROWAN JELLY

1.4 kg (3 lbs) rowan-berries
6 cloves
450 g (1 lb) cooking apples
1.1 L (2 pints) water
1 lemon rind only
Granulated sugar

Pick the rowan-berries from their stalks and put them into a preserving pan with the apples which have been roughly chopped. Add the lemon rind, cloves and the water. Simmer gently for about 1 hour or until the fruit becomes soft. Strain through a jelly bag and leave for several hours or overnight.

Then, measure the juice into the rinsed preserving pan, allowing 450 g (1 lb) sugar to 600 ml (l pint) juice, and stir over a gentle heat until the sugar has dissolved. Bring to the boil, and boil rapidly for 10 minutes. Draw the pan from the heat, test for setting and pour into small, warmed jars. Cover and seal them in the normal way.

Wild strawberries are not very common at this end of Skye, but occasionally a few may be found in sheltered woodland areas or grassy banks. The nearest equivalent in a cultivated form is the *alpine strawberry* and this has been known to grow very well in sunny, well-drained soil.

Because of their rarity and delicate flavour, I think the simpler way to serve them is the better.

WILD STRAWBERRIES WITH ORANGE

Place the strawberries in a pretty serving bowl, sprinkle them with caster sugar and leave to stand for 15 minutes. Then add the juice of 1 or 2 oranges, let stand for a further 30 minutes and serve with freshly whipped cream.

WILD STRAWBERRY AND PEACH CUPS *(Serves 4)*

2 large, fresh peaches
As many wild strawberries as you have been able to find
25 g (1 oz) caster sugar
50 ml (2 fl oz) kirsch

Plunge the peaches into boiling water and remove their skins. Slice in half, remove and discard their stones, and place in 4 individual glass dishes. In a separate bowl, mix the strawberries with the sugar and kirsch, and carefully pile into the centre of each peach.

Serve with freshly whipped cream and a finger of shortbread. (See page 135.)

This is recommended by herbalists as a soothing bed time drink.

WILD STRAWBERRY LEAF TEA

Pick the leaves in mid summer and lay on trays in the airing cupboard or a similarly warm dry place until curled and brittle. Crush with a rolling pin and store in an airtight jar.

To make the tea: infuse 2 tsps. dried leaves in 300 ml (½ pint) boiling water, add a pinch of thyme and sweeten with honey to taste.

HEBRIDEAI
MINERAL WATEI
STOP

Apart from the enjoyment of cooking, the kitchen range has many valuable uses, it heats the water, airs the clothes, keeps the kettle on the boil for that always welcome cup of tea and above all, provides warmth and comfort during the long winter evenings. The cats have always made the rocking chair close to the fire their permanent territory, and the dogs love to stretch full length on the hearth rug, creating keen competition for all! The kitchen is the most frequently used room in the house and is where visitors can relax and feel at home, whatever the time of day.

The cutting of peat for fuel has been a tradition of the island people for as long as history recalls, and from the time I first came to live here, I resolved to incorporate this valuable activity into my daily life. The weather largely determines when the cutting begins, but usually it is around the middle of April when the evenings are longer and there is good drying in the wind and sun.

Before the advent of the car, going to the peaks would be a day's outing for the whole family. Scones and sandwiches were made up the night before so as to provide everyone with refreshment, and on a fine day, with several irons cutting and plenty of helping hands to spread the peats out to dry, one household might cut enough for the whole year. The next stage came two or three weeks later when they were lifted into small heaps to let the underside dry and before harvesting began in July would be carried home in creels, or taken to the track and brought back with the pony and cart.

Today, with modern transport, most of us can be out on the hill within a quarter of the time it used to take, so the need to make a day's outing is no longer as necessary. For my part, I take the bicycle and with the dogs running alongside and a flask of tea in my rucksack, follow the track to the lighthouse. There is an open hill area of good black peat about ten minutes ride away, and after some initial help to remove the first layer of turf, I am content to cut, spread and stack, whilst listening to the song of the skylark and glancing now and again at the fine view across the Minch to the islands of Uist and Harris.

At the end of the summer, preferably before the August rain, I try to get the peats brought home by tractor and trailer. Then all that remains to be done is to make a stack by the garden gate and feel grateful an important job is over for another year.

So now for some ideas on how to use the kitchen range for baking.

Experimenting with yeast can be one of the most exciting aspects of baking – if you are not too daunted by it – and bread-making has always been as much a part of my daily life as all the other contributing elements mentioned in this book. With the nearest baker nine miles away, there is even more reason to be resourceful in this respect, and I can honestly say I have not bought a single loaf for my own consumption since the day I came here. It is not the difficult process so many imagine it to be, and after the initial mixing of the dough, which takes no longer than making a scone, you can leave it to prove whilst doing the housework, peeling the potatoes for lunch or carrying out any other task you have in mind. I usually make bread in the evenings whilst weaving, or writing letters, but everyone discovers their own time.

For those who feel like me that good home baked bread is the staff of life, here are a few well tested recipes for you to try.

(N.B. As fresh yeast is often difficult to come by I use Alinson's dried yeast, but this may be substituted for one sachet of the quick-acting variety if preferred.)

TRADITIONAL WHOLEMEAL BREAD *(Makes 2 loaves)*

675 g (1 ½ lbs) wholemeal flour, or wholemeal and granary mixed
225 g (½ lb) strong white flour
2 tsp. salt
1 tsp. brown sugar
3 tsp. dried yeast
1 tbsp. treacle
Warm water, to mix

Mix the flours and salt together in a large bowl. Dissolve the sugar in 225 ml (8 fl oz) of warm water, then sprinkle over it the yeast and stand both in a warm place until the yeast begins to froth (this usually takes about 10 minutes).

Meanwhile, dissolve the treacle in a little boiling water and add sufficient cold water to reduce the temperature to a medium heat. Add this, together with the frothy yeast mixture, to the flour and salt and knead well, adding more water as required to make a soft but not sticky dough. Turn out on to a floured board and knead well for about 5 minutes. Return the dough to the bowl, cover with a cloth and stand in a warm place until doubled in bulk (this takes about 1 hour).

Turn out again on to a floured board, knock back, shape into loaves and place in two well-oiled and warmed loaf tins. Dampen the surface with a little warm water, then sprinkle over a teaspoon of oatmeal or porridge oats. Cover, and allow to rise at room temperature for about half an hour.

When the dough looks as if it is just rising above the top of the tin, place in a pre-heated oven, 375°F/190°C, and bake for about 50 minutes, or until the loaves are golden-brown and sound hollow to the touch when turned upside-down. Cool on a wire rack.

TRADITIONAL WHITE BREAD *(Makes 2 loaves)*

1 kg (2 lbs) strong white flour
2 tsp. salt
25 g (1 oz) butter
1 tsp. sugar
3 tsp. dried yeast
Warm water, to mix

Sift the flour and salt into a large bowl and add the butter, working it in with the fingertips. Dissolve the sugar in 225 ml (8 fl oz) water and sprinkle over it the yeast. Stand both in a warm place until the yeast begins to froth (approximately 10 minutes), then add the yeast mixture to the flour together with enough warm water to make a soft but not sticky dough. Turn this out on to a floured board, knead well for about 5 minutes, and then return to the bowl, cover with a cloth and leave in a warm place to double in bulk (this takes about 1 hour).

Turn out again on to the floured board, knock it back, shape into loaves and place in two well-oiled and warmed loaf tins. Cover, and leave to rise at room temperature for half an hour, or until the dough is just beginning to rise above the top of the tin. Place in a pre-heated oven, 375°F / 190°C, for about 50 minutes, or until golden-brown and sounds hollow to the touch when turned upside down. Cool on a wire rack.

For a crusty top, mix a little cornflour with cold water to make a paste, add boiling water, and just before the loaves are put into the oven, brush the glaze over the tops and sprinkle with poppy seeds.

This recipe was given to me by a friend from South Africa:

SCHAAGEN VALLEY WHOLEWHEAT BREAD

7 cups coarse wholewheat flour
2 cups plain white flour
2 tsp. salt
1 cup sunflower seeds
1 tsp. sugar
3 tsp. dried yeast
1 tbsp. honey
4 cups warm water

Put the flours, salt and sunflower seeds into a large bowl. Dissolve the sugar in 1 cup of the water and sprinkle with the yeast. Stand both together in a warm place until the yeast becomes frothy (this takes about 10 minutes). Then add the honey to the yeast mixture, stirring well, and pour this, together with the remaining 3 cups of warm water, into the flour, kneading them together well.

Divide the dough, place in two well-oiled loaf tins, cover with a cloth and place in a warming oven for 1 hour. Then remove the cloth, turn up the heat to 375°F/190°C and cook for 1 hour. Cool on a wire rack.

This slightly sweet nutty bread is delicious for any occasion, and particularly good with soup and cheese.

RYE BREAD

450 g (1 lb) rye flour
450 g (1 lb) wholemeal flour
2 tsp. salt
25 g (1 oz) butter
1 dsp. caraway or cumin seeds
1 tsp. brown sugar
300 ml (½ pint) warm water
150 ml (¼ pint) milk
3 tsp. dried yeast
2 dsp. treacle
4 dsp. natural yoghurt

Put both the flours and salt into a bowl, rub in the butter with the fingertips and add the caraway or cumin seeds. Dissolve the sugar in the warm water, sprinkle over it the yeast and stand both in a warm place until the yeast is frothy (this takes about 10 minutes).

Next, heat the milk, dissolve in it the treacle, allow to cool a little and then stir it into the flour together with the yeast mixture and the yoghurt. Mix well, then turn out on to a floured board and knead for about 5 minutes. Return to the bowl, cover with a cloth and leave in a warm place to double in bulk (this takes about 1 ½ hours). Turn out again on to a floured board, shape into two rounds; then, dampen the tops with a little water, sprinkle with the caraway or cumin seeds and leave to rise in a warm place for about 30 minutes. Bake in a pre-heated oven at 425°F / 210°C for 30–40 minutes. Cool on a wire rack.

The dense quality of the rye flour means this bread takes longer to rise than most, but don't despair: it's very good to eat in the end.

50 g (2 oz) of sunflower seeds may be added – or *substituted* for the caraway or cumin seeds.

This recipe was given to me by a friend whilst I was travelling in New Zealand:

FLOWER-POT BREAD

4 ½ cups flour (wholemeal and white, mixed)
2 tbsp. wheatgerm
2 tsp. salt
1 tbsp. dried yeast
1 tsp. sugar
1 tbsp. oil

Put the flour, wheatgerm and salt in a bowl. Dissolve the sugar in 1 cup of warm water, sprinkle over the yeast and stand both in a warm place until the yeast is frothy. Pour the yeast mixture into the flour with the oil, adding more water if necessary, and knead together well on a floured board for about 5 minutes. Place in a well-oiled, 'clean' flowerpot, cover with a loosely tied plastic bag and allow to rise until doubled in bulk. Remove bag, and bake on the middle shelf of a pre-heated oven, 425°F/210°C, until well-risen and golden-brown. Turn out immediately and cool on a wire rack.

PITTA BREAD *(Makes 4 pittas)*

225 g (8 oz) wholemeal flour
25 g (1 oz) oatmeal
1 tbsp. wheatgerm
1 tsp. salt
½ tsp. sugar
150 ml (¼ pint) warm water
1 heaped tsp. dried yeast
1 tbsp. oil

Put the flour, oatmeal, wheatgerm and salt into a bowl. Dissolve the sugar in the warm water, sprinkle over the yeast and stand both in a warm place until the yeast is frothy (this takes about 10 minutes).

Now combine the yeast mixture with the flour, add the oil, mix together well, then turn out on to a floured board and knead well for about 5 minutes. Return to the bowl, cover with a cloth and leave in a warm place until doubled in bulk (this takes about 1 hour). Then, turn out again on to a floured board, divide into small balls and pat out, shaping into long ovals. Place on an oiled baking sheet, cover and leave to rise for 20 minutes.

Bake in a pre-heated oven at 400°F/200°C for 10 minutes. Then cool on a wire and rack and slit open with a sharp knife.

For an extra-crunchy finish, sesame seeds can be sprinkled over the top of each pitta bread before being left to rise for the second time.

GARLIC BREAD

For the bread:
450 g (1 lb) strong white flour
1 tsp. salt
½ tsp. sugar
225 ml (8 fl oz) warm water
2 tsp. dried yeast
15 g (½ oz) lard

For the garlic butter:
100 g (4 oz) butter
1-2 cloves garlic
Pinch of salt

Put the sifted flour and salt into a bowl. Dissolve the sugar in the warm water and sprinkle over the yeast. Stand both in a warm place until the yeast is frothy (this takes about 10 minutes). Then, rub the cooking fat into the flour with the fingertips and pour over the yeast mixture. Work together well, then turn out on to a floured board and knead for about 5 minutes. Return to the bowl, cover and leave in a warm place to double in bulk (this takes about 1 hour).

Turn out once more on to the floured board, knock back and briefly knead, then return to the bowl and leave to rise for about 30 minutes. Turn on to the floured board, and shape into a long stick. Place the dough on an oiled baking sheet, make small slashes slantwise along the surface, then cover with a cloth and leave to rise for 20 minutes. Brush with cold water and bake in a pre-heated oven at 400°F/200°C for 30-35 minutes. Cool on a wire rack.

To make the garlic butter, beat together the butter, crushed cloves of garlic and the salt until well mixed and smooth. Partially slit the bread in oblique slices about 2.5 cm (1 inch) thick, and butter each side with the butter mixture. Wrap in the foil and bake in a pre-heated oven at 400°F/200°C for 15-20 minutes.

Serve in the foil, as this helps to keep it hot.

GRANARY ROLLS

350 g (12 oz) granary flour
100 g (4 oz) strong white flour
1 tsp. salt
300 ml (½ pint) milk and water, mixed
1 tsp. light brown sugar
2 tsp. dried yeast
25 g (1 oz) butter

Put the two flours into a bowl with the salt. Gently heat the milk and water, dissolve the sugar and sprinkle it with the yeast. Stand in a warm place until the yeast is frothy (this takes about 10 minutes).

Rub the butter into the flour with the fingertips, and pour over the yeast mixture. Work together well, then turn on to a floured board and knead well for 5 minutes. Cover, and put in a warm place to double in bulk (this takes about 1 hour). Turn out again on to a floured board and knock back.

Divide the dough in half, then divide each half into 6 pieces. Knead each piece into a round, and place on an oiled baking sheet. Cover and leave in a warm place to rise for 20 minutes. Dust with flour, and place in a pre-heated oven, 425°F/220°C, for 15 minutes.

Serve warm with soup, or take on a picnic filled with cheese and chutney.

HERB AND GARLIC ROLLS

6 tbsp. milk
1 tbsp. sugar
1 tsp. salt
25 g (1 oz) butter
2 tsp. dried yeast
6 tbsp. warm water
150 g (5 oz) granary flour
150 g (5 oz) strong white flour
1 clove garlic
½ tsp. dried dill
1 tsp. dried rosemary

Scald the milk, dissolve in it the sugar, salt and butter, then cool to lukewarm. In a large bowl dissolve the yeast in the warm water, add the cooled milk, flour, (crushed) garlic and herbs. Work together well, then turn out on a floured board and knead for 5 minutes. Cover with a cloth and leave in a warm place to double in bulk (this takes about 1 hour).

Turn out again on to a floured board, knock back and divide the dough into 9-10 even-sized pieces. Knead each piece into a round, and then place on an oiled baking sheet, dampen a little with warm water and sprinkle with sesame seeds. Cover, leave to rise for about 20 minutes and then bake in a pre-heated oven at 425°F/210°C for 15 minutes. Cool on a wire rack.

APRICOT AND SULTANA BREAD

450 g (1 lb) strong white flour
225 ml (8 fl oz) milk and water, mixed
25 g (1 oz) sugar
1 tbsp. dried yeast
1 tsp. salt
1 tsp. mixed spice
25 g (1 oz) butter
1 egg
50 g (2 oz) dried apricots
50 g (2 oz) sultanas
25 g (1 oz) chopped walnuts (optional)

Sift 100 g (4 oz) of the flour into a small bowl. Slightly warm the milk and water, stir in 1 tsp. of the sugar and sprinkle over the yeast. Add to the flour, beat well until smooth and stand in a warm place for about 20 minutes until frothy.

Meanwhile, sift the rest of the flour and the sugar, together with the salt and the mixed spice, into a larger bowl, and put this also in a warm place until the yeast is ready. Now rub the butter into the flour with the fingertips, and add the yeasted mixture, beaten egg, chopped apricots, sultanas and walnuts. Mix thoroughly together, then turn out on to a floured board and knead for about 5 minutes. Return to the bowl, cover with a cloth and put in a warm place to double in bulk (this takes about 1 hour).

Turn out again on a floured board, knock back and shape into a loaf. Place in a well-oiled and warmed loaf tin, then cover and leave to rise for 30 minutes. Place in a pre-heated oven, 400°F/200°C, for 35 minutes, or until golden-brown and firm to the touch when turned upside-down. Glaze, whilst still hot, with a little sugar and milk that has been boiled together in a pan for a few minutes. Leave to cool completely on a wire rack.

If this bread gets a little stale, it is delicious when toasted.

DANISH COFFEE BUNS

350 g (12 oz) strong white flour
1 tsp. salt
170 ml (6 fl oz) milk
1 dsp. sugar
2 tsp. dried yeast
25 g (1 oz) butter
1 egg

Sift the flour and salt into a bowl. Gently heat the milk to lukewarm, dissolve in it 1 tsp. of the sugar and sprinkle over it the yeast. Stand together in a warm place until the yeast is frothy. Then rub the butter into the flour with the fingertips and add the remaining sugar. Pour in the yeast mixture and the beaten egg, work thoroughly together, then turn out on to a floured board and knead for 5 minutes. Cover with a cloth and leave in a warm place until doubled in bulk, (this takes about 1 hour).

Turn out again on to a floured board and divide the dough into small pieces. Knead each one into a round and place on an oiled baking sheet. Cover, let rise for 15 minutes, then brush with a little beaten egg or milk. Bake in a pre-heated oven at 400°F / 200°C for 10-15 minutes and then cool on a wire rack.

Eat warm with butter.

CHELSEA BUNS

450 g (1 lb) strong white flour
1 tsp. salt
½ tsp. mixed spice
½ tsp. cinnamon
225 ml (8 fl oz) milk
50 g (2 oz) sugar
1 tbsp. dried yeast
50 g (2 oz) butter
1 egg

For the filling:
75 g (3 oz) mixed dried fruits
¼ tsp. nutmeg
½ tsp. mixed spice

Sift the flour, salt and spices in a bowl. Slightly warm the milk, dissolve in it one tsp. of the sugar, sprinkle over it the yeast and then stand together in a warm place until the yeast is frothy (this takes about 10 minutes). Rub the butter into the flour with the fingertips, add the yeast mixture and the beaten egg, and work thoroughly together. Turn out on to a floured board, knead for 5 minutes and then cover and leave in a warm place until doubled in bulk (this takes about 1 hour). Turn out again on to a floured board, knock back and shape into an oblong about 40 × 30 cm (16 × 12 inches).

Mix the ingredients for the filling, and spread on the dough, patting in gently. Roll up the dough, starting at the long side, and moisten the edge with water to seal it. Cut into 2.5 cm (1 inch) slices and place separately, cut-side uppermost, on an oiled baking sheet. Cover with a cloth, put in a warm place to rise for about 15 minutes and then place in a pre-heated oven, 400°F/200°C, for 20 minutes.

Whilst still hot, brush with a glaze made by boiling together a little milk and sugar, or leave to get cold and cover with a thin layer of vanilla or lemon glacé icing.

FRUIT BUNS

450 g (1 lb) strong white flour
250 ml (9 fl oz) milk and water, mixed
50 g (2 oz) sugar
2 tsp. dried yeast
1 tsp. salt
½ tsp. mixed spice
½ tsp. cinnamon
50 g (2 oz) butter
1 egg
50 g (2 oz) currants
50 g (2 oz) sultanas
25 g (1 oz) mixed peel

Sift 100 g (4 oz) of the flour into a bowl. Slightly warm the milk and water, dissolve in it 1 tsp. of the sugar and then sprinkle over this the yeast. Sift together the remaining 350 g (12 oz) of flour, salt and spices, and stir in the remaining sugar. Stand both in a warm place until the yeast is frothy. Melt the butter, beat the egg, add both to the yeast mixture, combine all these with the spiced flour and the fruit and then blend thoroughly together. Then, turn out on to a floured board, knead for 5 minutes, cover with a cloth and put in a warm place to double in bulk (this takes about 1-1 ½ hours).

Turn out again on to a floured board, knock back and divide the mixture into 12 pieces. Shape into buns and place on a lightly floured greased baking sheet. Cover with a cloth, leave to rise in a warm place for about 15 minutes and then bake in a pre-heated oven at 375°F / 190°C for 15-20 minutes.

Whilst still hot, brush with a glaze made from a little sugar and milk boiled together for a few minutes. Cool on a wire rack.

SODA BREAD

175 g (6 oz) wholemeal flour
50 g (2 oz) plain white flour
25 g (1 oz) wheatgerm
25 g (1 oz) oatmeal
1 rounded tsp. bicarbonate of soda
1 rounded tsp. cream of tartar
½ tsp. salt
25 g (1 oz) butter
225 ml (8 fl oz) sour milk, or
  an equal amount of milk and natural yoghurt

Sift all the dry ingredients in a bowl and work in the butter with the fingertips. Make a well in the centre and gradually add the sour milk (or the milk and yoghurt, mixed together). Turn out on to a floured board, knead for a few seconds, and then shape into a round or oval, flatten a little and place on a floured baking tray. Using a sharp knife, make a deep cross in the centre, and bake in a preheated oven at 400°F/200°C for 35-40 minutes.

To make *white* soda bread, omit the wholemeal flour, oatmeal and wheatgerm and make up the difference with plain white flour.

WHOLEMEAL AND DATE SCONES

225 g (8 oz) wholemeal and white flour, mixed
A good pinch of salt
2 tsp. baking powder
25 g (1 oz) butter
25 g (1 oz) sugar
50 g (2 oz) dates
150 ml (¼ pint) sour milk, or
slightly less than ¼ pt milk with 2 tbsp. natural yoghurt

Sift the flour into a bowl with the salt and baking powder and rub in the butter with the fingertips. Add the sugar and the dates which have been roughly chopped, then add the sour milk (or milk and yoghurt mixed together), enough to make a soft but not sticky dough. Turn out on to a floured board, knead lightly and roll out to a thickness of 1 cm (½ inch). Then cut into squares or triangles and place on a floured baking tray. Place in a pre-heated oven 425°F / 190°C, for 10-12 minutes. Cool on a wire rack, or eat, whilst still hot, with plenty of butter.

TREACLE SCONES

225 g (8 oz) self-raising flour
½ tsp. bicarbonate of soda
A pinch of salt
25 g (1 oz) butter
1 dsp. sugar
1 tbsp. treacle
150 ml (¼ pint) milk

Sift the flour, bicarbonate of soda and salt into a bowl and rub the butter in with the fingertips; then stir in the sugar. Melt the treacle in a saucepan with the milk, allow to cool then add to the flour and mix to a softish dough. Turn out onto a floured board and roll out to a 1 cm (½ inch) thickness. Cut into rounds with a pastry cutter, place on a floured baking sheet and bake in a pre-heated oven at 425°F / 210°C for 10-15 minutes. Cool on a wire rack.

POTATO SCONES

225 g (½ lb) cold potatoes
15 g (½ oz) butter
Salt
About 50 g (2 oz) flour

Mash the potatoes, melt the butter and mix together well, adding salt and as much flour as is needed to make a paste. Roll out on to a floured board as thinly as possible, cut into rounds, place on a hot girdle or heavy frying pan that has been lightly greased, prick well and cook for 3 minutes on each side. Cool in a towel.

I have never been very good at making pancakes, but, seeing as they are such a traditional tea-time treat all over Scotland, I am including this recipe which was given to me by a local lady:

PANCAKES

1 cup sugar
2 eggs
2 ½ cups self-raising flour
1 tsp. cream of tartar
1 tsp. bicarbonate of soda
Milk, to mix
A knob of melted butter

Put the sugar and eggs in a bowl and beat well until thick and pale. Add the sifted flour with the cream of tartar and the bicarbonate of soda and mix together with sufficient milk to make a dropping consistency. Add the butter and beat well.

Heat and lightly grease a girdle or heavy frying pan, then drop spoonfuls of the mixture onto the hot surface. When bubbles appear, turn the mixture and cook for a further minute on the other side. Then place inside a folded cloth. Repeat this process until all the batter is used up.

BARA BRITH

100 g (4 oz) soft brown sugar
225 g (8 oz) mixed dried fruits
1 cup cold tea
2 eggs
1 tsp. mixed spice
225 g (½ lb) self-raising wholemeal flour

Soak the sugar and fruit in the cold tea overnight. Add the beaten eggs, spice and the flour. Mix together well and pour into a greased and lined loaf tin. Bake in a pre-heated oven at 350°F / 180°C for 1-1 ½ hours. Leave to cool for a few minutes, turn out on to a wire rack and leave to get completely cold.

This loaf keeps for several days if wrapped in foil or stored in an airtight tin.

ISLAY LOAF

150 g (6 oz) sultanas or raisins
100 g (4 oz) soft dark brown sugar
1 tbsp. treacle
25 g (1 oz) butter
300 ml (½ pint) water
275 g (10 oz) self-raising wholemeal and white flour, mixed
2 tsp. bicarbonate of soda
2 tsp. mixed spice
50 g (2 oz) chopped walnuts

Place in a saucepan the fruit, sugar, treacle, butter and water. Bring slowly to the boil, stirring frequently, then draw off the heat and allow to get almost cold. Fold in the sifted flour, bicarbonate of soda, mixed spice and the walnuts. Mix together well, then pour into a greased loaf tin and bake in a pre-heated oven at 350°F / 180°C for 1 hour.

Leave to cool in the tin for a few minutes, then turn out on to a wire rack and allow to get completely cold before storing in an airtight tin.

This is another loaf that keeps well.

As an alternative, I like to replace the mixed spice with ground ginger and the walnuts with 25 g (1 oz) chopped, crystallised ginger. Dates may also be substituted for the sultanas.

APRICOT AND WALNUT MALT LOAF

75 g (3 oz) dried apricots
2 tbsp. malt extract
50 g (2 oz) butter
50 g (2 oz) soft brown sugar
225 g (8 oz) self-raising wholemeal and white flour, mixed
1 tsp. baking powder
¼ tsp. salt
50 g (2 oz) walnuts
1 egg
6 tbsp. milk

Place the apricots in a bowl, cover with cold water and leave to soak for 2 hours. Then, drain and roughly chop.

Put the malt, butter and sugar in a saucepan and heat gently until the butter is melted and the sugar dissolved. Sift the flour, baking powder and salt into a separate bowl, and then add the cooled malt mixture, the apricots, walnuts and, lastly, the egg and milk, which have been beaten together well. Stir carefully, then beat until smooth.

Pour the mixture into a greased loaf tin and place in a pre-heated oven, 325°F/170°C for 50-60 minutes. Allow to cool in the tin for 10 minutes, then turn out on a wire rack to get completely cold.

This loaf keeps well if wrapped in foil or stored in an airtight tin.

DATE AND ORANGE LOAF

225 g (8 oz) dates
110 ml (4 fl oz) water
50 g (2 oz) soft brown sugar
50 g (2 oz) butter
1 egg
Grated rind 1 orange, and 2 tbsp. its juice
225 g (8 oz) self-raising wholemeal and white flour, mixed
1 tsp. cinnamon
¼ tsp. freshly grated nutmeg

Put the dates and the water in a saucepan, simmer gently until soft, then add the sugar and stir until dissolved. Remove from the heat and directly add the butter beating in well. Cool a little, then beat in the egg, orange rind and juice, the sifted flour, cinnamon and nutmeg. Pour into a greased loaf tin and bake in a pre-heated oven at 350°F/180°C for 1 hour. Leave to cool in the tin for a few minutes, then turn out on to a wire rack to get completely cold.

This loaf is better kept for a few days before eating, and keeps well stored in an airtight tin.

BANANA AND WALNUT LOAF

100 g (4 oz) butter
100 g (4 oz) soft brown sugar
100 g (4 oz) self-raising wholemeal flour
100 g (4 oz) self-raising white flour
1 tsp. bicarbonate of soda
225 g (½ lb) ripe bananas
2 eggs
A few drops vanilla essence
50 g (2 oz) walnuts
2 tbsp. boiling milk

Cream the butter and sugar until light and fluffy. Sift the two kinds of flour together with the bicarbonate of soda into a separate bowl. Mash the bananas. Beat the eggs and add a little at a time to the creamed butter mixture, add the bananas alternately with a spoonful of flour. When the flour is all used up add the walnuts, milk and the vanilla essence and pour into a greased and lined loaf tin.

Bake in a pre-heated oven at 350°F / 180°C for 1 hour, allow to cool for a few minutes, and then turn out on to a wire rack and leave to get completely cold. This loaf is better kept for a few days before eating, and keeps well stored in an airtight tin.

One year, I had a cooking job on St Kilda for the month of May, and this old family recipe was given to me by my neighbour for the hungry helpers working for the National Trust. It can either be served as a pudding, or sliced cold to have with a cup of tea.

CLOOTIE DUMPLING

1 kg (2 lbs) self-raising flour
225 g (8 oz) shredded suet
1 level tbsp. bicarbonate of soda
1 tsp. mixed spice
1 tsp. cinnamon
350 g (¾ lb) demerara sugar
2 large cooking apples (grated)
675 g (1 ½ lbs) sultanas or raisins (or mixed)
3 heaped tbsp. syrup
3 heaped tbsp. treacle

Put the flour into a bowl with the suet and mix together well. Then, add all the other ingredients except for the syrup and treacle. Melt these in a saucepan separately, then pour over the flour mixture together with enough water to make a fairly soft dough.

Put a large cloth into a bowl of hot water, wring it out thoroughly, then lay it out flat and sprinkle liberally with flour. Place the dough in the centre, and tie the edges together firmly, leaving enough room for the dumpling to swell. Then put it on a plate, and place in the bottom of a large saucepan, adding enough boiling water to cover. Simmer for 3-4 hours.

Turn it out carefully, and eat hot or cold.

FARMHOUSE FRUIT CAKE

225 g (8 oz) butter
225 g (8 oz) soft light brown sugar
4 large eggs
225 g (8 oz) plain white flour
A pinch of salt
100 g (4 oz) raisins
100 g (4 oz) sultanas
50 g (2 oz) mixed peel
50 g (2 oz) glacé cherries
A few drops of vanilla essence
Milk to mix

Grease and line a 20 cm (8 inch) cake tin. Cream the butter and sugar together until light and fluffy. Then, beat the eggs and add them alternately (to the butter and sugar) with a spoonful of the sifted flour, and salt. When all the flour is used up, add the raisins, sultanas, mixed peel, vanilla essence and the cherries (which have been washed, dried and cut into quarters). Mix together well, adding enough milk to make the mixture soft but not wet then place in the prepared tin, level with a knife and make a small depression in the centre.

Place in the centre of a pre-heated oven, 350°F / 180°C, for 30 minutes, and then reduce the heat to 300°F / 160°C and continue cooking for 1 hour. Allow to cool in the tin for 30 minutes, then turn out on to a wire rack and leave to get completely cold. Store in an airtight tin and keep for at least one day before eating.

FRUIT GINGERBREAD

100 g (4 oz) margarine
100 g (4 oz) black treacle
100 g (4 oz) golden syrup
150 ml (¼ pint) milk
2 eggs

225 g (8 oz) plain flour
50 g (2 oz) sugar
1 tbsp. ground ginger
1 tsp. bicarbonate of soda
100 g (4 oz) sultanas

Grease and line a tin 18 × 28 cm (7 × 11 inches). Put the margarine, treacle and syrup in a saucepan, heat gently, add the milk and leave to cool slightly. Then beat in the eggs.

Sift dry ingredients into a bowl, add the treacle mixture and beat well until smooth. Stir in the sultanas, then pour into the prepared tin and place in a pre-heated oven at 300°F/150°C for about 40 minutes. Leave to cool in the tin for 30 minutes, then turn out on to a wire rack, and when completely cold wrap in tin foil or store in an airtight tin. Leave for two days before cutting.

This recipe was given to me by my mother, who in turn, had been given it by her mother. It was obviously not designed for an afternoon tea party, but was a good substantial stand-by for feeding hungry children!

SEED CAKE

450 g (1 lb) plain white flour
1 tsp. salt
2 tsp. baking powder
100 g (4 oz) dripping
2 heaped tsp. caraway seeds

100 g (4 oz) sugar
25 g (1 oz) mixed peel
1 egg
Milk to mix

Grease a 450 g (1 lb) loaf tin or a 20 cm (8 inch) round cake tin. Sift the flour, salt and baking powder into a bowl, rub in the dripping with the fingertips, and then add all the dry ingredients and bind together with the beaten egg and enough milk to form a soft dough. Place in the prepared tin and bake in a preheated oven at 350°F/180°C for 1 ½-2 hours. Allow to cool in the tin for a few minutes, then turn out on to a wire rack and leave to get completely cold before storing in an airtight tin.

If you have any left-over mincemeat at Christmas, I find the following recipe both useful and delicious.

CUT AND COME AGAIN CAKE

175 g (6 oz) butter
100 g (4 oz) soft brown sugar
3 eggs
200 g (8 oz) self-raising wholemeal and white flour mixed
1 tsp. baking powder
100 g (4 oz) mincemeat
100 g (4 oz) mixed dried fruits
1 tsp. vanilla essence

Grease and line a 7 or 8 inch (18 or 20 cm) round tin. Sift flour and baking powder into a bowl and set aside. Cream together the butter and sugar until light and fluffy, then beat in the eggs one at a time adding a little of the flour to prevent curdling. Add the mincemeat, the dried fruits, the rest of the flour and the vanilla essence and mix well together.

Place mixture in prepared tin, smooth the surface and make a small well in the centre. Bake in the centre of the oven at 350°F/180°C for 30 minutes, then reduce temperature to 325°F/160°C for 30 minutes, or until golden brown and a skewer placed in the middle of the cake comes out clean. Leave in the tin for 5 minutes before turning out on to a wire rack to cool completely. Store in an airtight tin. This keeps well for several weeks.

WHOLEMEAL CARROT CAKE with orange glacé icing

100 g (4 oz) butter
100 g (4 oz) soft light brown sugar
Grated rind 1 orange
175 g (6 oz) wholemeal self-raising flour
A pinch of salt
1 tsp. cinnamon
100 g (4 oz) grated carrots
2 large eggs
Milk, to mix

Glacé icing:
100 g (4 oz) icing sugar
Juice of 1 orange

Grease and line a 18 cm (7 inch) round cake tin. Cream the butter and sugar together until light and fluffy, and add the grated orange rind. Sift the flour, salt and cinnamon into a separate bowl, and add the grated carrot. Beat the eggs and add to the creamed butter mixture a little at a time, alternating with a spoonful of the flour-and-grated-carrot mixture until it is all used up. Add enough milk to make the mixture soft but not wet, and then bake in a pre-heated oven, 325°F/170°C, for 1 hour, or until a skewer comes out clean when inserted in the middle.

Allow to cool in the tin for a few minutes, then turn it out on to a wire rack and leave to get completely cold. Cover with the icing which has been made by combining sufficient orange juice with the sifted icing sugar to make a smooth paste. Decorate with walnut halves.

CHOCOLATE WALNUT SQUARES

100 g (4 oz) margarine
100 g (4 oz) soft light brown sugar
2 eggs
175 g (6 oz) self-raising flour
1 tbsp. cocoa powder
100 g (4 oz) chopped dates
50 g (2 oz) chopped walnuts
A few drops of hot water

Grease a small Swiss-roll tin. Cream the margarine and sugar until light and fluffy. Beat the eggs and add one at a time, alternating with a spoonful of the sifted flour and cocoa powder. Add the chopped dates and walnuts and just enough hot water to make a soft consistency. Put into the prepared tin, smooth over evenly with a knife and bake in a pre-heated oven at 350°F / 180°C for 20 minutes. Cool in the tin and, when cold, cut into squares. Store in an airtight tin.

Another old-fashioned recipe from my mother, often given to us as children:

ROCK CAKES

225 g (8 oz) plain flour
1 tsp. baking powder
½ tsp. salt
75 g (3 oz) dripping (or margarine will do)
50 g (2 oz) sugar
50 g (2 oz) currants
25 g (1 oz) peel
1 tsp. baking powder
Milk, to mix

Sift the flour, baking powder and salt into a bowl. Add the dripping (or margarine) and rub in with the fingertips. Add all the dry ingredients and mix to a stiff dough with the milk. Place in small heaps on a greased baking sheet using two forks, and then place in a pre-heated oven, 400°F / 200°C, for 15-20 minutes.

For a more modern version, I prefer to use wholemeal self-raising flour and to add one beaten egg to the mixture and to use less milk. A few chopped cherries or 1 tsp. of mixed spice can also be used as a variation.

This is a particularly good traditional recipe, given to me by Mary MacDonald, Edinbane:

OATCAKES

100 g (4 oz) good medium oatmeal (or pin head and medium oatmeal mixed)
½ tsp. salt
Pinch bicarbonate of soda
1 tsp. sugar
15 g (½ oz) butter
50-75 ml (2-3 fl oz) boiling water

Place the oatmeal in a small bowl with the salt, bicarbonate of soda and sugar. Put the butter in a saucepan with the boiling water, and when bubbling hot, pour enough over the oatmeal to make a wettish but binding paste. Mix well with a knife, then turn out on to a board that has been liberally covered with some extra oatmeal. Pat into a round, working the oatmeal into the top and sides, then with the palm of the hand, start kneading in a radial movement, turning the oatcake a little with each fresh knead. Do this until the dough becomes even and round and has a depth of about 3 mm (⅛ inch). Cut into triangles and place on a baking sheet. Place in a pre-heated oven at 350°F/180°C for 20-30 minutes turning each oatcake 5 minutes before the baking time is complete. Cool on a wire rack and store in an airtight tin.

They can be eaten with any accompaniment of your choice, but are best with either crowdie or honey.

FLAPJACKS

175 g (6 oz) margarine
75 g (3 oz) soft light brown sugar
1 dsp. treacle
1 dsp. golden syrup
225 g (8 oz) rolled oats
50 g (2 oz) coconut

Melt the margarine, sugar, treacle and syrup together in a saucepan over a gentle heat. Add the rolled oats and the coconut. Spread the mixture into a greased Swiss-roll tin (not too large) and bake in a pre-heated oven at 350°F/180°C for 20 minutes or until golden-brown.

Allow to cool a little, then cut into squares with a sharp knife and when completely cold remove and store in an airtight tin.

Sometimes, I add 50 g (2 oz) sultanas to the mixture just before baking.

These are similar to flapjacks, but with a fruity, nutty difference:

APRICOT CRUNCHES

50 g (2 oz) dried apricots
175 g (6 oz) margarine
1 tbsp. treacle
100 g (4 oz) demerara sugar
225 g (8 oz) rolled oats
50 g (2 oz) chopped hazelnuts or walnuts

Cover the apricots with boiling water, leave to soak for a few hours, then drain, wipe and roughly chop.

Place the margarine, treacle and sugar in a saucepan and stir until all the ingredients are melted. Remove from the heat and stir in the oats, apricots and chopped nuts. Spread the mixture into a greased Swiss-roll tin (not too large) and bake in a pre-heated oven at 350°F/180°C for 20 minutes or until golden-brown.

Allow to cool a little, then cut into squares with a sharp knife and when completely cold remove and store in an airtight tin.

Another recipe brought home from my travels in New Zealand:

MUESLI CHEW

1 egg
½ cup chopped dates
2 tbsp. soft brown sugar
½ cup mixed fruit
½ cup coconut
50 g (2 oz) butter
½ cup wholemeal flour
2 tbsp. honey
1 cup cornflakes
1 cup muesli

In a medium-sized bowl, beat the egg and sugar until thick and pale, then add the dry ingredients and the fruit mixing together well. Melt the butter and honey in a saucepan and add to the mixture. Press into a greased tin 18 × 28 cm (7 × 11 inches) and bake in a pre-heated oven at 350°F / 180°C for 20 minutes. When cool cut into squares and store in an airtight tin.

OATMEAL COOKIES

50 g (2 oz) soft brown sugar
200 g (7 oz) medium oatmeal
100 g (4 oz) wholemeal flour
½ tsp. bicarbonate of soda
1 tsp. mixed spice
75 g (3 oz) raisins
75 g (3 oz) butter
1 egg

Put the sugar, oatmeal, flour, bicarbonate of soda, mixed spice and raisins into a bowl, then melt the butter and pour this over, adding the beaten egg and mixing together well. Roll the mixture into small balls in the palm of the hand, and place well apart on a greased baking sheet. Flatten slightly with a fork and bake in a pre-heated oven, 350°F / 180°C for 10-12 minutes.

Cool for a little, then remove to a wire rack and when completely cold store in an airtight tin.

PEANUT COOKIES

75 g (3 oz) margarine
50 g (2 oz) soft brown sugar
100 g (4 oz) wholemeal flour
(or self raising wholemeal flour omitting the baking powder)
½ tsp. baking powder
50 g (2 oz) shelled peanuts

Cream the margarine and sugar together in a bowl until light and fluffy. Add the flour, baking powder and peanuts and mix well to blend. Form into balls, place on a greased baking sheet, leaving enough space in between for them to spread a little, then bake in a pre-heated oven 350°F/180°C for 15 minutes.

Cool for a little, then remove to a wire rack and when completely cold store in an airtight tin.

SESAME AND NUT BISCUITS

175 g (6 oz) margarine
75 g (3 oz) soft brown sugar
1 tbsp. treacle
50 g (2 oz) sesame seeds
50 g (2 oz) nuts
225 g (8 oz) wholemeal flour (or self raising wholemeal flour omitting the baking powder)
1 tsp. baking powder

Cream the margarine and sugar in a bowl until light and fluffy, then add the treacle and all the other ingredients, blending together well. Roll out on a floured board and cut into rounds with a pastry cutter. Place on a greased baking sheet and bake in a pre-heated oven at 350°F/180°C for 15-20 minutes. Cool for a little, then remove to a wire rack and when completely cold store in an airtight container.

ROSEMARY BISCUITS

100 g (4 oz) butter
50 g (2 oz) soft brown sugar
175 g (6 oz) wholemeal and plain white flour, mixed
1 tbsp. dried rosemary

Cream the butter and sugar together in a bowl until light and fluffy, then add the flour and the rosemary and knead with the hands until it forms a dough. Roll out on a floured board and cut into rounds with a pastry cutter. Place on a greased baking sheet and bake in a pre-heated oven at 400°F/200°C for 10-12 minutes, or until firm and golden-brown.

Cool for a little, then remove to a wire rack and when completely cold store in an airtight tin.

WALNUT BISCUITS

100 g (4 oz) margarine
50 g (2 oz) soft light brown sugar
A few drops vanilla
150 g (5 oz) plain white flour
50 g (2 oz) chopped walnuts

Cream the margarine and the sugar together in a bowl until light and fluffy. Add the vanilla essence, the sifted flour and then the walnuts. Knead lightly together until a dough is formed then turn out on to a floured board and roll out to a 0.5 cm (¼ inch) thickness. Cut into rounds with a pastry cutter and place on a greased baking sheet. Bake in a pre-heated oven at 350°F / 180°C for 15-20 minutes, or until golden brown. Cool for a little, remove to a wire rack and when completely cold store in an airtight tin.

TRADITIONAL SHORTBREAD

225 g (8 oz) slightly salted butter
100 g (4 oz) caster sugar
200 g (7 oz) plain flour
125 g (5 oz) cornflour

Cream the butter and sugar together in a bowl until light and fluffy, then add the sifted flour and the cornflour. Knead lightly and press into a Swiss-roll tin. Prick well and bake in a pre-heated oven, 300°F / 150°C for 1 hour or until pale golden-brown and firm to the touch.

With a knife mark into squares whilst still hot, then when cold cut completely, remove from tin and store in an airtight container.

CHOCOLATE SHORTBREAD

175 g (6 oz) butter
75 g (3 oz) dark soft brown sugar
150 g (5 oz) plain white flour
50 g (2 oz) cornflour
2 dsp. cocoa powder
100 g (4 oz) plain chocolate

Cream the butter and sugar together in a bowl until light and fluffy and then add the sifted flour, cornflour and cocoa powder. Knead together lightly and press into a greased Swiss-roll tin. Place in a pre-heated oven, 350°F / 180°C, for 25-30 minutes.

Grate the chocolate and, when the shortbread is cooked, scatter over the top and return to the oven for a minute; then remove and smooth over with a knife. Cool in the tin and then cut into slices. Store in an airtight tin.

ANULATED
NESUGAR

As a child, I remember family walks in the countryside collecting flowers and berries for my father to make into wine, and I suppose the happy memories that are conjured up have encouraged me to continue this pastime since coming to live in Skye. There is something very satisfying about being able to make your own inexpensive country wines - and to recall the occasion whilst gathering the produce.

The beginner should not be put off by the overwhelming terminology found in some books, for as long as you have a few pieces of simple equipment, a warm kitchen or airing cupboard and plenty of storage space for the finished wines to mature, the actual procedure is quite straight forward; and by following a few simple rules, you can not only enjoy the results, but also feel encouraged to make it a lasting hobby.

I find the easiest way to collect the material needed for wine is to hang a plastic pail over my arm and, with a 1 pint container, measure the flowers and berries as I go. A pair of scissors can be useful for snipping off heads and stems, and rubber gloves are essential for picking nettles!

It is important to choose a fine day, when flowers are fully open or berries recently ripened, for apart from ensuring a better bouquet to the wine, there is less likelihood of any bacteria being present, which can turn the wine sour during fermentation.

A guide to basic equipment is listed as follows:

At least two fermentation jars (more if you intend to make several wines)
1 air-lock and cork for each fermentation jar
1 new plastic pail
600 ml (1 pint) measuring jug
1 large plastic spoon
1 fine-mesh sieve, or an ordinary household one with a piece of fine muslin
A piece of siphoning tube for racking the wine
Campden tablets for sterilising
Wine bottles and corks

SPRING

I have listed the following wines in order of season, and have included those made with vegetables from my own garden.

DANDELION WINE

4.5 L (1 gallon) dandelion flowers (freshly picked, with the petals stripped from their stalks)
4.5 L (1 gallon) water
1.4 kg (3 lbs) granulated sugar
1 orange
1 lemon
25 g (1 oz) fresh yeast

Put the dandelion petals into a plastic pail and pour over 4.5 L (1 gallon) of boiling water. Leave covered for 10-12 days, stirring well once a day.

Strain the liquid into a preserving pan and add the sugar together with the thinly pared rinds of the orange and lemon. (Care should be taken not to include any white pith, as this will make the wine bitter.) Then, add the two fruits roughly chopped and bring the contents to the boil. Simmer gently for 20 minutes, then remove from the heat and cool to lukewarm. Spread the yeast on a piece of toast and leave to float on the top.

Cover with a cloth and leave in a warm place for 2 days. Strain the liquid into a fermentation jar, fit the airlock and leave for 2 months before racking. Rack again if required, and bottle in 6 months' time.

The idea of picking so many primrose blooms may upset some people, but remember it is only the *flowers* and not the roots that you will be taking; and besides, during a year when they are particularly prolific, such a cropping will hardly be noticed.

PRIMROSE WINE

4.5 L (1 gallon) primrose flowers
4.5 L (1 gallon) water
1.4 kg (3 lbs) sugar
1 orange
1 lemon
Wine yeast
1 tsp. yeast nutrient

Bring the water to the boil and stir in the sugar, making sure it is well dissolved. Put the finely pared rinds of the orange and lemon into a plastic pail, making sure not to include any white pith, and pour the hot syrup over the top. Allow to cool to lukewarm, then add the juice of the fruits, the primrose flowers, the yeast and the yeast nutrient. Stir well, cover closely and put in a warm place for 5 days, stirring each day.

Then, strain into a fermentation jar, fit the airlock and leave for 2-3 months before racking. Rack again as required, and bottle in 6 months' time.

GORSE FLOWER WINE

4.5 L (1 gallon) gorse flowers
4.5 L (1 gallon) boiling water
2 oranges
2 lemons
1.4 kg (3 lbs) sugar
2 tbsp. strong cold tea
Wine yeast
1 tsp. yeast nutrient

Put the flowers into a plastic pail, pour over the boiling water and leave to stand for 3 days, stirring each day.

Strain the liquid into a preserving pan and add the thinly pared orange and lemon rinds - making sure not to include any white pith – the juice from the fruit and the sugar. Bring to the boil and simmer gently for ¼ of an hour. Allow the liquid to cool to lukewarm, and then add the strong cold tea, the wine yeast and the nutrient. Stir well, cover closely and put in a warm place for 3 days, stirring occasionally. Then, strain into a fermentation jar, fit the airlock and leave for 2-3 months before racking. Rack again, and bottle after 6 months.

BROOM WINE

4.5 L (l gallon) broom flowers
4.5 L (l gallon) boiling water
1 orange
1 lemon
1.4 kg (3 lbs) demerara sugar
2.5 cm (1 inch) root ginger
Wine yeast
1 tsp. yeast nutrient

Put the flowers into a plastic pail, pour over the boiling water, cover and leave to stand for 3 days, stirring once a day.

Strain the liquor into a preserving pan, add the finely pared orange and lemon rinds - making sure not to include any white pith - the sugar and the ginger which has been bruised and tied in a muslin. Bring to the boil and simmer for quarter of an hour. Pour back into the plastic bucket and when cooled to lukewarm, add the yeast and the yeast nutrient. Stir well, cover closely and put in a warm place for 2 days. Strain into a fermentation jar, fit the airlock and let stand for 2-3 months before racking. Rack again and bottle after 6 months.

HAWTHORN FLOWER WINE

2.3 L (2 quarts) hawthorn flower
2 lemons
4.5 L (1 gallon) water
1.4 kg (3 lbs) sugar
2 tbsp. strong cold tea
Wine yeast
1 tsp. yeast nutrient

Thinly pare the lemons - being careful not to include any white pith - and bring to the boil with the water, sugar and the juice of one of the lemons. Simmer gently for 30 minutes, then pour into a plastic pail and cool to lukewarm. Add the strong cold tea, the wine yeast and the nutrient, stirring well, and then cover closely and put in a warm place for 24 hours. Add the flowers and leave to stand for a further 8 days, stirring well each day. Strain into a fermentation jar, fit the airlock and leave for 2-3 months before racking. Rack again and bottle after 6 months.

NETTLE WINE

2.3 L (2 quarts) young nettle tops
15 g (½ oz) root ginger
2 lemons
4.5 L (1 gallon) water
1.4 kg (3 lbs) sugar
Wine yeast

Wash the nettle tops and put in a preserving pan. Add the bruised ginger tied in a muslin, the thinly pared lemon rind and some of the water. Bring to the boil and simmer gently for 45 minutes. Strain into a plastic pail and make it up to 4.5 L (1 gallon) with more boiling water. Add the sugar and the juice of the lemons, stir well and when cooled to lukewarm, add the wine yeast and the nutrient. Cover closely and put in a warm place for 4 days. Stir thoroughly and transfer into a fermentation jar, fit the airlock and leave for 2-3 months before racking, then rack again and bottle after 6 months.

EARLY SUMMER

ELDERFLOWER WINE

4.5 L (1 gallon) elderflowers (no fleshy green stems)
Rind and juice of 3 lemons
4.5 L (1 gallon) water
1.5 kg (3½ lbs) granulated sugar
Wine yeast
Yeast nutrient

Put the flowerlets and thinly pared lemon rind into a plastic pail. Boil the water and sugar for 10 minutes, pour over the flowerlets and then add the lemon juice. Leave to stand until lukewarm and then add the yeast and the yeast nutrient, stirring well. Cover closely and put in a warm place for 14 days. Strain into a fermentation jar, fit the airlock and leave for 2-3 months before racking. Rack again and bottle after 6 months.

RHUBARB WINE

2.3 kg (5 lbs) rhubarb (best picked in May or June)
4.5 L (1 gallon) water
2 Campden tablets
Precipitated chalk
(this helps to neutralise the excess oxalic acid)
1 tsp. citric acid
2 tbsp. strong cold tea
1 tsp. yeast nutrient
1.4 kg (3 lbs) sugar
Wine yeast

Wash the rhubarb and cut into small pieces, slitting them lengthwise. Put into a plastic pail and cover with cold water, add the crushed Campden tablets. Stir twice daily for 10 days, then strain the liquid into another pail and add approximately 15 g (½ oz) precipitated chalk- this should be added *slowly*, and as soon as the fizzing stops, do not add any more (don't worry if it looks milky, this will clear during the fermentation). Now add the citric acid, the cold tea, the nutrient, sugar and finally the yeast. Pour immediately into a fermentation jar, fit the airlock and let stand for 2-3 months before racking. Rack again and bottle after 6 months.

ROSE PETAL WINE

I have a number of semi-wild rosebushes in my garden, and if I gather the petals when they are newly fallen, they can be used to make this light and fragrant wine.

2.3 L (2 quarts) rose petals (the stronger scented, the better)
4.5 L (8 pints) boiling water
1.1 kg (2½ lbs) granulated sugar
1 lemon
Wine yeast
Yeast nutrient

Put the rose petals into a plastic pail, pour over the boiling water and add the sugar and juice from the lemon. When it has cooled to lukewarm, add the yeast and the yeast nutrient. Cover closely and put in a warm place for 1 week, stirring daily.

Strain into a fermentation jar, fit the airlock and leave for 2-3 months before racking. Rack again and bottle after 6 months.

MID SUMMER

MEADOWSWEET WINE

1.1 L (2 pints) meadowsweet flowers (flowerlets only)
2 lemons
4.5 L (1 gallon) boiling water
1.4 kg (3 lbs) sugar
100 g (¼ lb) raisins
2 tbsp. strong cold tea
Wine yeast
1 tsp. yeast nutrient

Put the flowerlets in a plastic pail with the finely pared lemon rinds , pour over the boiling water and add the sugar and the raisins. Leave to cool until lukewarm, then add the lemon juice, strong cold tea, yeast and the yeast nutrient. Stir well then cover closely and put in a warm place for 10 days, stirring daily.

Strain into a fermentation jar, fit the airlock and leave for 2-3 months before racking. Rack again and bottle after 6 months.

GOOSEBERRY OR WORCESTERBERRY WINE

2.7 kg (6 lbs) gooseberries or worcesterberries – or the two mixed together
3.5 L (6 pints) boiling water
1.1 kg (2 ½ lbs) granulated sugar
Wine yeast
1 tsp. yeast nutrient

Wash and top and tail the gooseberries or worcesterberries and squeeze a little so that the juice starts to run. Put into a plastic pail and pour over the boiling water. Cover closely and leave to stand for 3 days, stirring occasionally.

Strain into another pail, add the sugar, stirring well until it has dissolved, and then add the yeast and yeast nutrient. Pour immediately into a fermentation jar, fit the airlock and leave for 2-3 months in a warm place before racking. Rack again and leave for 12 months.

BLACKCURRANT WINE

1.4 kg (3 lbs) blackcurrants
1.8 kg (4 lbs) granulated sugar
4.5 L (1 gallon) water
Wine yeast
1 tsp. yeast nutrient

Crush the blackcurrants and put them into a plastic pail. Boil up the sugar in the water and pour over the currants. When it has cooled to lukewarm, add the yeast and the yeast nutrient and keep well-covered in a warm place for 5 days, stirring occasionally.

Strain into a fermentation jar, fit the airlock, and leave to stand for 2-3 months before racking. Rack again, siphon into dark bottles (this helps to preserve the colour) and then keep for 12 months.

This unusual-sounding wine has an excellent flavour and is a useful way of using up surplus pea pods, if you are not wanting them for the compost heap:

PEA POD WINE

2.3 kg (5 lbs) pea pods
4.5 L (1 gallon) water
1.4 kg (3 lbs) granulated sugar
1 tbsp. citric acid
1 tbsp. strong cold tea
Wine yeast
1 tsp. yeast nutrient

Wash the pods carefully, and then boil them in the water until they are tender. Strain the liquid into a plastic pail and dissolve in it the sugar, stirring well. When cooled to lukewarm, add the citric acid, strong cold tea, yeast and yeast nutrient. Pour immediately into a fermentation jar, fit the airlock and leave to stand in a warm place for 2 months before racking. Rack again and bottle after 6 months.

AUTUMN

ROWAN-BERRY WINE

2.3 L (½ gallon) rowan-berries
4.5 L (1 gallon) boiling water
1.5 kg (3 ½ lbs) sugar
450 g (1 lb) raisins
225 g (½ lb) wheat
Wine yeast
1 tsp. yeast nutrient

Put the rowan-berries into a plastic pail and pour over the boiling water. Let it stand for 4 days, then strain into a fresh plastic pail and add the sugar, chopped raisins and wheat, stirring well until the sugar has dissolved; then add the yeast and the yeast nutrient. Cover closely and leave to ferment for 16 days in a warm place. Strain into a fermentation jar, fit the airlock and leave for 2-3 months before racking. Rack again and bottle after 6 months.

This wine improves when kept for at least 12 months before drinking.

It is not very often that we find fully ripened elderberries in the north end of Skye. Either there is not sufficient sunshine, or a late-summer gale takes most of them away. I usually collect mine from either the south end of the island or the Mainland.

ELDERBERRY WINE

1.8 kg (4 lbs) ripe elderberries
4.5 L (1 gallon) boiling water
Wine yeast
1 tsp. yeast nutrient
1.5 kg (3 ½ lbs) granulated sugar

Strip the berries from their stalks with a fork, and crush them in a plastic pail. Pour on the boiling water and let cool to lukewarm before adding the yeast and the yeast nutrient. Cover closely and leave to stand for 3 or 4 days, stirring daily.

Then, strain on to the sugar (which has been put in another container), stir until dissolved and pour into a dark fermentation jar and fit the airlock (do not fill completely until the first ferment has subsided). Leave for about 3 months before racking, rack again in 3 months and siphon into dark bottles and keep for at least 12 months before drinking.

The dark fermentation jar and bottles used in this recipe are necessary for preserving the colour.

BRAMBLE WINE

2.7 kg (6 lbs) brambles
4.5 L (1 gallon) boiling water
1.4 kg (3 lbs) sugar
Wine yeast
1 tsp. yeast nutrient

Wash the brambles and put in a plastic pail. Pour over the boiling water, cover closely and let it stand for 3 days, stirring occasionally.

Strain into another container, add the sugar, yeast and the yeast nutrient, and stir well until the sugar has dissolved. Pour into dark fermentation jar and fit the airlock (do not fill completely until the first fermentation has subsided). Leave for about 3 months and siphon into dark bottles and keep for at least 12 months before drinking.

The dark fermentation jar and bottles used in the recipe are important for preserving the colour.

WINTER

BEETROOT WINE

1.4 kg (3 lbs) beetroot
4.5 L (1 gallon) water
1.4 kg (3 lbs) sugar
Juice 1 lemon
6 cloves
25 g (1 oz) bruised ginger
Wine yeast
1 tsp. yeast nutrient

Wash the beetroots well (but do not peel), cut them up and boil them in some of the water until tender but not mushy. Strain on to the sugar, the lemon juice and spices which have been placed in a pail, add the remaining boiling water, stir until the sugar is dissolved and leave until lukewarm. Add the yeast and the yeast nutrient, cover closely and leave in a warm place for 3 days, stirring each day.

Strain into a dark fermentation jar, fit the airlock and let stand for about 3 months before racking. Rack again and after 6 months, siphon into dark bottles and keep for 12 months before drinking.

The dark fermentation jar and bottles used in this recipe are important for preserving the colour.

CARROT WINE

2.7 kg (6 lbs) carrots
4.5 L (1 gallon) water
1.8 kg (4 lbs) sugar
2 lemons
2 oranges
1 tbsp. raisins
450 g (1 lb) wheat
1 tsp. dried yeast

Wash the carrots well but do not peel. Put them into a preserving pan, cover with the water, bring to the boil and then simmer gently until the carrots are tender. Strain into another container and make up to the gallon with boiling water. Then, add the sugar and sliced lemons and oranges, and stir well until the sugar has dissolved. Leave until lukewarm, then add the chopped raisins, the wheat and the 1 tsp. dried yeast. Cover closely and leave in a warm place for 15 days, stirring once daily. Strain into a fermentation jar, fit the airlock and let stand until it is clear and stable. If the lees build up to more than 2 cm (¾ inch), rack and before finally bottling, rack again.

This wine is best kept for at least 1 year before drinking.

PARSNIP WINE

1.8 kg (4 lbs) parsnips (after peeling)
4.5 L (1 gallon) water
25 g (1 oz) root ginger
2 lemons
1.4 kg (3 lbs) granulated sugar
25 g (1 oz) fresh yeast

Chop the parsnips into small pieces and put in a plastic pail with the water, bruised ginger and the sliced lemons. Let it stand for 24 hours. Then pour into a preserving pan and bring to the boil. Simmer until the parsnips are tender but not too soft, and then strain on to the sugar in a plastic pail, stir well and allow to cool. When lukewarm, add the yeast (spread on a piece of toast), cover closely and leave to stand in a warm place for 12 hours.

Strain into a fermentation jar, fit the airlock and leave for about 3 months in a warm place before racking. Rack again and leave for 12 months before drinking.

This recipe was given to me by a Sussex lady who lived in the village where I was studying weaving. It is one of my favourites:

WHEAT AND RAISIN WINE

600 ml (1 pint) whole-wheat grains
1 kg (2 lbs) raisins
1.8 kg (4 lbs) demerara sugar
1 large potato
4.5 L (1 gallon) boiling water
1 orange
1 lemon
25 g (1 oz) fresh yeast

Put the wheat, raisins, sugar and grated and peeled potato into a plastic pail and pour on the boiling water. Put in the sliced orange and lemon and when it has all cooled to lukewarm spread the yeast on a piece of toast and float it on the top. Cover closely and leave to stand in a warm place stirring each day for 21 days.

Strain into a fermentation jar and fit the airlock. Let stand for about 2-3 months and then rack, repeating the racking as necessary before bottling.

Keep for at least 9 months before drinking.

AUTHOR'S NOTE

It was during a tour of the Highlands in the summer of 1965 that I first came to Skye. I thought then what a beautiful island it was, but not until returning some years later for a camping and hill-walking holiday with a friend did the magic totally cast its spell, and in the Autumn of 1977 I found myself accepting the winter-let of a cottage on a north-facing peninsula, with six months to find out if I could survive and earn myself a living.

English-born, with a number of years spent travelling to different parts of the world, I had for some while considered the possibility of setting up my own handweaving business in the Highlands, making use of local wool and the wide variety of plants for dyeing, whilst benefiting from the summer tourist trade for selling my products. I worked hard through that first experimental winter, weaving a variety of items for the Easter visitors and maintaining financial independence by gathering winkles from the shore and by taking on a part-time cleaning job at the village school. I felt secure and at ease with my newly found life. So, when Spring came and there was a possibility of purchasing the last croft house at the end of the road, I felt ready to put in my offer and planned on making this my permanent home.

The weaving orders and sales continued to keep me busy throughout most of the year; there was seldom any shortage of work and indeed, often a rush to get the last orders posted and the new stock on display for the following season. In July and August, when the meadowsweet, tansy and ragwort were in bloom, a large dyeing would be done, and in Autumn any fleeces collected during the annual shearing had to be washed, dried and put into bags ready for winter use. Each task perpetuated its own natural cycle and just like the garden, there was a season for everything.

For ten years the pattern of life changed very little, but then as the economics began to prove I was no longer earning a realistic living, it seemed inevitable I should look for an additional income and so it was that I turned to cooking.

Fortunately, with a little experience gained from preparing meals for friends salmon-fishing each September, and having spent a month on St Kilda catering for parties involved with restoration work for the National Trust, I was able to make use of this knowledge to secure further work and I now spend a number of weeks throughout the year cooking in lodges for six or more people who are fishing, stalking or simply enjoying a family holiday in remote parts of the Highlands.

Christmas and New year are other busy times when people invariably want help with the festive celebrations, and in Skye there is the occasional business lunch and house party when meals are either cooked on the premises or prepared at home and delivered when required.

It was whilst I was cooking for the musicians at Dunvegan Castle during the Chamber Music Festival in 1989 that the idea for this book was first conceived. Their appreciation and enthusiasm for locally grown foods using fresh fruit and vegetables from my garden was a great compliment and encouragement, and so, although hesitant at first to undertake such a project, once persuaded I enjoyed selecting recipes using ingredients I can grow or gather, and compiling the contents which I hope will bring pleasure to others.

A special mention is given to the artist and illustrator Judith MacLachlan whom I have known since my early years on the island, when we shared weaving and dyeing experiments together. Nowadays, she is involved mainly in drawing and print-making, and it has been a great privilege to combine her ideas with mine in the making of this book.

ACKNOWLEDGEMENTS

A special thank you goes to Robert Arnold for his patience and help with the word-processor during the many hours spent compiling and correcting this book, also to his wife Anne for reading the text and giving her support.

Gratitude is warmly extended to the writer and food critic Derek Cooper for his interest at the early stages of the book's development and for offering to write the Foreword.

I would like to express my thanks to Mary MacDonald who read the text and donated two of her favourite recipes, to Donald MacLachlan who initially instructed me on how to use the word-processor, to Hugh MacLeod of Dunvegan Castle who provided the photograph for the back cover and lastly to my neighbour Norah MacLean who imparted to me the knowledge of local history and tradition, without which the book would have lost much of its essence.

INDEX